A BRIEF RETOLD VERSION OF
TRUE INDIAN MYTHOLOGY

RAMAYANA

A BRIEF RETOLD VERSION OF
TRUE INDIAN MYTHOLOGY

RAMAYANA

Authored by
NEERAJ SHARMA

Office No. 03, Guru Harkishan Nagar,
Paschim Vihar, Delhi, 110087
Website: www.authorlandselfpublishing.com
Email: publish@authorlandselfpublishing.com

First Published by Authorland Self Publishing 2023
Copyright © Neeraj Sharma 2023
All Rights Reserved.

Title: Ramayana
Price: ₹399 | $9.99
ISBN: 978-81-963253-0-5

DEDICATION

This book is dedicated to the timeless tale of the Ramayana, and to the rich heritage of Indian mythology, this book is dedicated. May its retelling bring the ancient wisdom and profound teachings of the epic to new generations, igniting their imagination and fostering a deep connection with our cultural roots. With gratitude, it is dedicated to the divine characters and their eternal significance, the sages and scholars who have preserved this sacred narrative, and to all those who hold the Ramayana close to their hearts, embracing its timeless values of righteousness, devotion, and the triumph of good over evil.

CONTENTS

PREFACE

Welcome to "Ramayana: A Brief Retold Version of True Indian Mythology." In this book, we embark on a journey through the timeless epic of the Ramayana, exploring its rich mythology, profound teachings, and enduring relevance in our lives today.

The Ramayana is an ancient Indian epic that holds a special place in the hearts of millions around the world. It is a captivating tale of love, devotion, valor, and the eternal battle between good and evil. Through its vivid characters, dramatic events, and profound wisdom, the Ramayana has been a guiding light for generations, imparting valuable life lessons and inspiring millions to strive for righteousness and spiritual growth.

In this retold version, we aim to present the essence of the Ramayana in a concise and accessible manner, making it accessible to readers of all ages and backgrounds. While maintaining the integrity and authenticity of the original epic, we have condensed its vast narrative into a concise yet powerful retelling, capturing the key events, characters, and teachings that make the Ramayana such a timeless masterpiece.

Within the pages of this book, you will encounter the noble and righteous Prince Rama, his loyal brother Lakshmana, the virtuous Sita, and the enigmatic Hanuman, among many other iconic characters. You will witness the divine intervention, epic battles, and the triumph of good over evil. But beyond the action and adventure, the Ramayana offers profound insights into human nature, relationships, duty, and the eternal quest for spiritual enlightenment.

It is important to note that the Ramayana is not just a mythological tale; it is a profound source of wisdom and inspiration. The characters and events in the epic represent universal truths and ideals that continue to resonate with readers across cultures and generations. The teachings of the Ramayana, such as devotion, sacrifice, loyalty, and the power of righteousness, hold valuable lessons for navigating the complexities of modern life.

In retelling the Ramayana, we have strived to bring its essence to life while staying true to its original spirit. We hope that this book serves as a gateway to the profound world of Indian mythology, igniting your curiosity and inspiring you to delve deeper into its vast treasure trove of stories and teachings.

As you immerse yourself in the pages of this retold version of the Ramayana, we invite you to open your heart and mind to its timeless wisdom. Allow the epic to transport you to a world of gods and demons, of love and heroism, and of the eternal struggle between good and evil. May it inspire you to embody the virtues of truth, righteousness, and compassion in your own life, and may it awaken within you a deeper appreciation for the rich tapestry of Indian mythology.

We extend our gratitude to the ancient sages and scholars who preserved the Ramayana through generations, as well as to the artists, poets, and translators who have brought its beauty to life in various forms. It is their collective efforts that have kept this profound epic alive and relevant in our modern times.

We hope that "Ramayana: A Brief Retold Version of True Indian Mythology" sparks a sense of wonder and curiosity in you, and that it serves as a gateway to a deeper exploration of the epic and the rich cultural heritage it represents. May it inspire you to embrace the timeless teachings of the Ramayana and embark on your own quest for spiritual growth and self-discovery.

Wishing you an enriching and transformative journey through the pages of this retold version of the Ramayana.

Neeraj Sharma
Founder, Director & CEO
Authorland Self Publishing LLP

The Epic Tale of Ramayana

THE SIGNIFICANCE OF RAMAYANA IN INDIAN MYTHOLOGY

The Ramayana holds immense significance in Indian mythology, representing the rich cultural and spiritual heritage of the country. It is not merely a story but a revered scripture that has shaped the values, beliefs, and traditions of millions of people for centuries.

CULTURAL IDENTITY

The Ramayana is deeply ingrained in the cultural fabric of India. It reflects the ideals and virtues cherished by Indian society, such as righteousness, devotion, loyalty, and familial duty. The characters of Lord Rama, Sita, Hanuman, and others have become iconic figures symbolizing moral excellence and spiritual strength.

MORAL AND ETHICAL TEACHINGS

The Ramayana serves as a moral compass, offering valuable lessons on dharma (righteousness) and the ethical conduct of individuals. It emphasizes the importance of upholding truth, honoring promises, respecting elders, and fulfilling one's duties. The epic encourages individuals to live a life of virtue and integrity.

DEVOTION AND BHAKTI

The Ramayana evokes deep devotion and love for Lord Rama and Sita. It inspires millions of devotees to follow the path of bhakti (devotion) towards God. Through the story of Lord Rama's unwavering love for his wife Sita and his divine qualities, the Ramayana ignites the flame of devotion in the hearts of believers.

ARCHETYPAL CHARACTERS

The Ramayana presents a range of characters that represent various archetypes and personalities. Lord Rama embodies the ideal king and the embodiment of virtue, while Sita symbolizes purity, loyalty, and feminine strength. Hanuman, the devoted monkey god, represents unwavering loyalty and dedication. These characters resonate with individuals and provide inspiration for personal growth and self-discovery.

EPIC BATTLE OF GOOD VS. EVIL

The Ramayana showcases the eternal battle between good and evil. Lord Rama's quest to rescue Sita from the clutches of the demon king Ravana highlights the triumph of righteousness over darkness. The epic teaches the importance of standing up against injustice and fighting for what is right.

SYMBOLISM AND ALLEGORY

The Ramayana is replete with symbolism and allegorical elements that convey deeper philosophical truths. The characters, events, and locations in the epic often have symbolic meanings. For example, the city of Ayodhya represents an ideal kingdom, while the forest symbolizes the challenges and tests of life. These allegories provide profound insights into the human condition and the spiritual journey.

INFLUENCE ON LITERATURE AND ARTS

The Ramayana has been a tremendous source of inspiration for literature, poetry, music, dance, and visual arts across various cultures and time periods. It has given birth to numerous adaptations, retellings, and artistic expressions, both in India and beyond. The epic's themes of love, heroism, sacrifice, and divine intervention continue to captivate artists and audiences alike.

SOCIAL AND ETHICAL VALUES

The Ramayana imparts valuable social and ethical values that shape the conduct of individuals and society. It emphasizes the importance of upholding familial relationships, respecting elders, honoring one's word, and valuing the well-being of the community. The epic fosters a sense of unity, compassion, and harmony within society.

SPIRITUAL SIGNIFICANCE

The Ramayana serves as a spiritual guide, offering profound insights into the nature of reality and the path to liberation. It explores concepts of karma, dharma, devotion, and the divine play of gods and goddesses. The epic inspires individuals to seek a deeper connection with the divine and embark on a spiritual journey of self-realization.

TIMELESS RELEVANCE

Despite being thousands of years old, the Ramayana remains relevant in contemporary times. Its teachings on morality and ethics transcend time and continue to resonate with people from all walks of life. The lessons of compassion, integrity, and righteousness taught in the Ramayana are universal and hold relevance in navigating the complexities of modern society.

BRIEF OVERVIEW OF THE CHARACTERS AND PLOT

The Ramayana, one of the most celebrated and revered epics in Indian mythology, tells the timeless tale of love, duty, and the triumph of good over evil. Let us take a brief overview of the key characters and plot that make this epic so captivating and enduring.

The protagonist of the Ramayana is Lord Rama, the seventh avatar of Lord Vishnu. Known for his unwavering devotion to righteousness, Rama is portrayed as the ideal king, husband, and son. His journey forms the central narrative of the epic. Rama's consort and beloved wife, Sita, is a symbol of purity, loyalty, and feminine strength. Her abduction by the demon king Ravana sets the course for the epic's events.

Ravana, the primary antagonist, is a powerful and intelligent demon king who rules over the island of Lanka. Driven by his desire for Sita, Ravana kidnaps her, leading to a fierce battle between him and Lord Rama. Ravana represents the forces of evil, while Rama embodies righteousness and dharma.

The epic also features several notable characters who play significant roles in shaping the narrative. Hanuman, the loyal and devoted monkey god, becomes Rama's staunch ally and plays a pivotal role in the rescue of Sita. His unwavering devotion, strength, and intelligence make him a beloved figure in Hindu mythology.

Other important characters include Lakshmana, Rama's loyal brother who accompanies him on his journey and serves as his right-hand man. Bharata, Rama's half-brother, who takes on the responsibilities of ruling Ayodhya in Rama's absence. Sita's steadfast and protective companion, Jatayu, who tries to rescue her from Ravana but is ultimately defeated.

The plot of the Ramayana revolves around Rama's exile from his kingdom, Ayodhya, and his quest to rescue Sita. Rama, along with Lakshmana and an army of vanaras (monkey warriors) led by Hanuman, embarks on a perilous journey across forests, mountains, and mythical realms. They encounter various challenges, battles, and divine beings along the way.

The epic encompasses themes of love, honor, sacrifice, and the battle between good and evil. It explores the concepts of duty, devotion, and the consequences of one's actions. The Ramayana is not merely a story of heroic deeds but also a profound philosophical and spiritual discourse that delves into the nature of existence, human relationships, and the divine play of gods and goddesses.

The climax of the Ramayana is the epic battle between Rama and Ravana. It is a monumental clash that showcases Rama's valor, strategy, and divine assistance from beings like Hanuman and the monkey army. In the climactic battle, Rama eventually defeats Ravana, rescues Sita, and restores dharma and righteousness.

The Ramayana concludes with Rama's triumphant return to Ayodhya, where he is reunited with his loved ones and ascends to the throne as the rightful king. His reign is considered a golden age, symbolizing the victory of righteousness and the establishment of a just and harmonious society.

The Ramayana, with its rich tapestry of characters and compelling plot, continues to captivate readers and inspire countless adaptations, retellings, and artistic expressions. It serves as a moral compass, guiding individuals towards the path of righteousness, devotion, and selflessness.

Through the Ramayana, we are reminded of the eternal values of love, honor, and the indomitable spirit of good. It teaches us the importance of fulfilling our duties, upholding moral principles, and embracing the power of righteousness in our lives. The Ramayana is a timeless epic that not only entertains and captivates readers, but also imparts profound wisdom and moral teachings that hold relevance in today's world. It serves as a guiding light, offering valuable insights into the human condition and the complexities of life.

The characters in the Ramayana represent various aspects of human nature, allowing readers to relate to their struggles, triumphs, and inner conflicts. Lord Rama embodies the qualities of a noble and just leader, teaching us the importance of righteousness and honor in our actions. Sita, with her unwavering faith and resilience, inspires us to face adversity with grace and dignity. Hanuman's devotion and loyalty remind us of the power of unwavering faith and selfless service.

The plot of the Ramayana is a gripping saga of love, betrayal, sacrifice, and redemption. It explores the eternal battle between good and evil, reminding us of the choices we make and their consequences. Through Rama's exile, the challenges he faces, and the ultimate victory of righteousness, we learn the importance of staying true to our values even in the face of adversity.

Beyond its narrative, the Ramayana offers profound philosophical and spiritual insights. It delves into the nature of karma, the significance of duty, and the complex dynamics of relationships. It teaches us the value of selflessness, compassion, and forgiveness, and encourages us to lead a life of purpose and integrity.

The Ramayana has left an indelible mark on Indian culture and has influenced literature, art, music, and dance for centuries. Its teachings have been passed down through generations, shaping the moral fabric of society. Its timeless wisdom continues to inspire individuals from all walks of life, transcending boundaries of time, culture, and religion.

CHAPTER ONE

The Prophecy of Lord Rama's Birth

THE PROPHECY OF LORD RAMA'S BIRTH

The prophecy of Lord Rama's birth is a significant aspect of the Hindu epic, the Ramayana. It foretells the arrival of a divine incarnation, destined to restore righteousness and vanquish evil forces. This prophecy not only sets the stage for the epic tale but also highlights the divine plan and purpose behind Lord Rama's advent.

According to the ancient scriptures, the prophecy originates from the celestial realm, where the gods and sages foresee the growing imbalance and turmoil on Earth. The universe, witnessing the increasing atrocities committed by demons and the need for divine intervention, responds by orchestrating Lord Rama's birth.

The prophecy states that Lord Rama would be born as the eldest son of King Dasharatha and Queen Kausalya of Ayodhya, an ancient city in present-day India. The king, an upright and virtuous ruler, is chosen by the gods to be the father of this divine incarnation. The prophecy also reveals that Lord Rama's purpose is to restore righteousness (dharma) and uphold moral values in the world.

The divine seer, Sage Vishvamitra, recognizes the significance of this prophecy and approaches King Dasharatha with a request. He seeks the assistance of young Rama and his brother Lakshmana in protecting the sacrificial rituals from the demons who seek to disrupt them. King Dasharatha, aware of the divine nature of his sons, happily agrees, setting in motion a series of events that lead to Lord Rama's heroic journey.

The prophecy's importance lies not only in the identity and purpose of Lord Rama but also in the impact it has on the characters and events throughout the Ramayana. It creates a sense of anticipation, as the birth of Lord Rama holds the promise of deliverance from evil and the restoration of peace and harmony.

The prophecy also emphasizes the divine nature of Lord Rama's incarnation. It signifies his connection to the divine realm and his role as the chosen instrument of Lord Vishnu, the preserver of the universe. Lord Rama's birth is seen as a divine intervention in response to the prayers and pleas of the gods, who seek to restore order and justice on Earth.

The prophecy's fulfillment is marked by extraordinary celestial occurrences. As Lord Rama takes birth, the heavens celebrate with showers of flowers, celestial music, and divine beings descending to witness this momentous event. The entire universe seems to rejoice, recognizing the arrival of the divine incarnation.

The prophecy holds deep symbolism and spiritual significance. It represents the eternal struggle between good and evil, righteousness and injustice, and the divine intervention that ensures the triumph of virtue. Lord Rama's birth is seen as a beacon of hope in times of darkness, offering solace and inspiration to all those who strive for righteousness.

Moreover, the prophecy serves as a reminder of the cyclical nature of life and the concept of divine incarnations in Hindu mythology. Lord Rama's birth is not an isolated event but part of a grand cosmic plan, wherein the divine takes human form to restore order and guide humanity on the path of righteousness.

The prophecy also highlights the power of faith and devotion. It demonstrates the unwavering belief of the gods, sages, and devotees in the divine plan, as they eagerly anticipate Lord Rama's arrival. Their faith serves as a testament to the profound impact that devotion can have in invoking the grace of the divine and bringing about positive transformation.

In summary, the prophecy of Lord Rama's birth is a pivotal element in the Ramayana, laying the foundation for the epic tale of righteousness, valor, and the triumph of good over evil. It signifies the divine plan to restore harmony in the world and serves as a reminder of the power of faith, devotion, and the eternal struggle between light and darkness.

CHILDHOOD STORIES AND ADVENTURES OF LORD RAMA

The childhood stories and adventures of Lord Rama, as depicted in the Hindu epic Ramayana, are enchanting tales that reveal the divine nature, exceptional qualities, and extraordinary feats of this revered deity. These narratives not only showcase Lord Rama's playful and mischievous nature but also provide valuable lessons in morality, bravery, and devotion.

Lord Rama, born as the eldest son of King Dasharatha and Queen Kausalya of Ayodhya, had a blissful and idyllic childhood. From an early age, he exhibited remarkable qualities that set him apart from others. Lord Rama was compassionate, gentle, and possessed an innate sense of righteousness that captivated the hearts of all who came into contact with him.

One of the most renowned childhood stories of Lord Rama is the episode of him breaking the divine bow of Lord Shiva. King Janaka of Mithila organized a grand ceremony where suitors from far and wide attempted to string the powerful bow, with the condition that the one who succeeded would win the hand of his daughter, Princess Sita. Lord Rama, in his playful innocence, effortlessly lifted and broke the bow, stunning everyone present and leaving them in awe of his strength and divinity.

Lord Rama's adventures extend beyond his hometown of Ayodhya. One notable journey was the visit to the hermitage of Sage Vishvamitra. Accompanied by his faithful younger brother, Lakshmana, Lord Rama embarked on this expedition, which would prove to be a turning point in their lives. During their time in the hermitage, the brothers encountered numerous demons and wicked beings that threatened the peace of the sage's abode. Lord Rama fearlessly battled these evil forces, showcasing his courage, valor, and dedication to protecting the righteous.

Another captivating tale from Lord Rama's childhood is the story of the Golden Deer. While residing in the forest during his exile, Sita, Lord Rama's beloved wife, expressed her desire to possess the enchanting and elusive golden deer. To fulfill her wish, Lord Rama set out to capture the magical creature. Little did he know that it was a cunning trick orchestrated by the demon king Ravana to distract Lord Rama and abduct Sita. This episode showcases Lord Rama's unconditional love for his wife and the lengths he was willing to go to ensure her happiness.

Lord Rama's encounters with various celestial beings during his childhood further add to the allure of his adventures. One such encounter was with Lord Hanuman, the mighty monkey god who would become Lord Rama's devoted disciple and trusted ally. Their first meeting, filled with awe and wonder, laid the foundation for a lifelong bond of friendship and unwavering loyalty. Lord Rama recognized Hanuman's exceptional qualities and realized that he would play a pivotal role in his divine mission.

Lord Rama's childhood stories also highlight his humility and compassion for all living beings. There is a famous anecdote of him befriending the lowly tribal boy, Guha, who became an ardent devotee and offered his unwavering support to Lord Rama. This narrative underscores Lord Rama's ability to transcend societal boundaries and embrace the inherent divinity in all individuals, regardless of their social status.

Moreover, Lord Rama's childhood adventures in the Ramayana serve as a moral compass for devotees. They emphasize the importance of adhering to dharma (righteousness) and upholding moral values in the face of adversity. Lord Rama's unwavering commitment to truth, his respect for elders, and his compassion towards all creatures serve as timeless lessons that continue to inspire individuals in their daily lives.

In conclusion, the childhood stories and adventures of Lord Rama in the Ramayana are captivating narratives that not only entertain but also impart profound lessons in morality, bravery, and devotion. Lord Rama's playful and mischievous nature, coupled with his divine qualities, make his childhood tales enchanting and relatable.

Through his feats, Lord Rama exemplifies the virtues of righteousness, compassion, courage, and humility. Whether it is breaking the divine bow, battling demons in the hermitage, or befriending celestial beings like Hanuman, Lord Rama's actions demonstrate his unwavering commitment to upholding dharma and protecting the righteous.

These stories also emphasize the power of love, loyalty, and familial bonds. Lord Rama's love for his wife Sita is evident in his pursuit of the golden deer, and his unwavering dedication to her safety and well-being. His brother Lakshmana's unwavering loyalty and devotion serve as an example of the deep bond of brotherhood.

Lord Rama's encounters with various celestial beings and his interactions with individuals from different walks of life highlight his acceptance and inclusivity. His friendship with Guha, the tribal boy, showcases his ability to see beyond social boundaries and treat all beings with respect and compassion.

Furthermore, Lord Rama's childhood adventures in the Ramayana teach us the importance of adhering to dharma and moral values. They remind us of the significance of truth, righteousness, and compassion in our daily lives. Lord Rama's character serves as a role model, inspiring us to navigate challenges with courage and integrity.

These childhood stories of Lord Rama have not only captivated audiences for centuries but also influenced art, literature, and cultural traditions. They continue to be retold and celebrated in various forms, including theater, dance, and festivals, deepening the understanding and devotion towards Lord Rama.

Ultimately, the childhood stories and adventures of Lord Rama in the Ramayana serve as a source of inspiration, moral guidance, and spiritual enlightenment. They convey timeless values and lessons that are relevant to people of all ages and backgrounds. Lord Rama's divine qualities, his playful nature, and his heroic deeds continue to resonate with devotees, reminding us of the power of righteousness, love, and devotion in overcoming obstacles and leading a fulfilling life.

CHAPTER TWO

The Marriage of Lord Rama and Sita

THE SWAYAMVAR OF SITA

The Swayamvar of Sita is one of the most significant events in the epic Ramayana, where the noble princess Sita chooses her life partner amidst a gathering of powerful and worthy princes. This event not only portrays the virtues of Sita but also reveals the qualities of Lord Rama, who ultimately emerges as the victor and the chosen one.

The Swayamvar is a traditional ceremony in which a bride selects her groom from a group of suitors who have gathered to win her hand. In the context of the Ramayana, it becomes a pivotal moment that determines the course of the epic tale. The Swayamvar of Sita is known for its grandeur, the complexity of its tasks, and the underlying message of true love and devotion.

Princess Sita, renowned for her beauty, grace, and virtuous qualities, captivates the hearts of all who lay eyes upon her. Her father, King Janaka, devises a unique challenge for the suitors, setting an unbreakable bow as the condition for winning Sita's hand in marriage. Many powerful and accomplished princes attempt to wield the bow, but none succeed.

Amidst the crowd of princes, Lord Rama stands out as the epitome of perfection. His demeanor, radiance, and divine aura make him an undeniable candidate for Sita's hand. Lord Rama, accompanied by his faithful brother Lakshmana, approaches the mighty bow with utmost humility and reverence.

As Rama grasps the bow, the atmosphere becomes charged with anticipation. With his unparalleled strength and grace, Rama effortlessly lifts the bow, stringing it to its breaking point. The sound resonates through the assembly, leaving everyone in awe of his might. The bow, which has remained unyielding in the hands of countless others, succumbs to the power and righteousness of Lord Rama.

The breaking of the bow not only signifies Rama's physical strength but also symbolizes his unwavering devotion, righteousness, and ability to overcome any obstacle. It is through this act that Rama proves himself as the perfect match for Sita, deserving of her hand in marriage. The assembled kings and princes, recognizing Rama's valor and divine qualities, acknowledge his victory with admiration and respect.

The Swayamvar of Sita serves as a powerful metaphor for the search for a worthy life partner and the significance of true love and compatibility. It highlights the importance of virtue, integrity, and righteousness in a relationship. Sita's choice of Rama is not solely based on physical strength or external qualities but on the alignment of their values, character, and spiritual connection.

The Swayamvar also showcases the immense respect and admiration that Sita holds for Rama. It is a testament to her unwavering faith in him and her recognition of his divine nature. Sita's decision to choose Rama as her husband demonstrates her understanding of his greatness and her willingness to embark on a lifelong journey of love, devotion, and sacrifice.

Furthermore, the Swayamvar of Sita is a significant moment in the Ramayana as it sets the stage for the subsequent events and challenges that Rama and Sita must face together. It symbolizes the beginning of their divine union and their role as the embodiment of ideal love, companionship, and partnership.

In conclusion, the Swayamvar of Sita in the Ramayana is a momentous event that showcases the virtues of Sita and the divine qualities of Lord Rama. It portrays the power of true love, devotion, and righteousness in determining a life partner. The breaking of the unbreakable bow by Rama not only establishes his physical strength but also signifies his unwavering commitment to upholding dharma. The Swayamvar of Sita is a significant event in the Hindu epic Ramayana, portraying the strength, wisdom, and devotion of the characters involved. This ancient tradition of choosing a life partner through a challenging task highlights the importance of compatibility, character, and divine intervention.

The Swayamvar takes place in the kingdom of Mithila, ruled by King Janaka, Sita's father. The event attracts princes and noble warriors from far and wide, all vying for the chance to win Sita's hand in marriage. King Janaka, aware of Sita's exceptional qualities, devises a test to determine the most deserving suitor.

The centerpiece of the Swayamvar is a mighty bow, known as the Shiva Dhanush, which can only be lifted and strung by the most powerful of men. The bow is said to be a divine weapon of Lord Shiva himself, making it an object of immense significance and difficulty. Princes attempt to lift the bow, but one after another, they fail in their endeavors.

Enter Lord Rama, the seventh avatar of Lord Vishnu, accompanied by his loyal brother Lakshmana. Rama's arrival at the Swayamvar creates a stir among the gathering, as his reputation as a noble prince and his divine aura precede him. With grace and humility, Rama approaches the Shiva Dhanush, and to the astonishment of all, effortlessly lifts and strings the mighty bow.

The moment Rama accomplishes this feat, the Swayamvar hall resonates with a sense of awe and reverence. The celestial beings and the assembled guests are captivated by Rama's divine presence. Sita, observing the unfolding scene, recognizes Rama as her destined life partner and offers her garland of acceptance to him.

The Swayamvar of Sita signifies not just physical strength, but the embodiment of qualities that make a worthy spouse. Rama's ability to lift the Shiva Dhanush symbolizes his unmatched power, righteousness, and unwavering commitment to dharma (righteousness). Sita's choice of Rama is a testament to her discernment, recognizing his virtues and divine nature.

This event also highlights the deep spiritual connection between Rama and Sita. Their union is not merely based on external appearances or material wealth but on their shared devotion to righteousness, love, and their divine purpose. The Swayamvar showcases the significance of a harmonious partnership built on shared values and a commitment to each other's growth and well-being.

The Swayamvar of Sita also holds broader philosophical implications. It demonstrates the importance of aligning oneself with divine will and following the path of righteousness. Rama's success in lifting the bow illustrates that divine intervention plays a crucial role in determining the course of our lives and that true strength lies in surrendering to the higher power.

Furthermore, the Swayamvar serves as a turning point in the Ramayana, setting the stage for Rama and Sita's journey together and the trials they will face. It symbolizes their union as an ideal couple, where their love, devotion, and unwavering support for each other become the foundation for their eventual triumph over evil.

In essence, the Swayamvar of Sita is a testament to the power of virtue, righteousness, and divine intervention. It emphasizes the importance of character, compatibility, and the recognition of one's divine purpose in the search for a life partner. Through the Swayamvar, Rama and Sita's union becomes a shining example of love, devotion, and the triumph of righteousness over adversity.

THE BREAKING OF SHIVA'S BOW AND LORD RAMA'S MARRIAGE

The Breaking of Shiva's Bow and Lord Rama's Marriage is a significant event in the Hindu epic Ramayana, marking the union of Lord Rama and Sita and setting the stage for their extraordinary journey. This event showcases the valor, skill, and devotion of Lord Rama and demonstrates the divine intervention that guided their path.

The story unfolds in the kingdom of Ayodhya, ruled by King Dasharatha, where the sage Vishwamitra seeks Rama's assistance in vanquishing the demons that trouble his hermitage. Rama, accompanied by his loyal brother Lakshmana, agrees to accompany the sage and protect the sacred rituals.

On their way to the hermitage, Rama and Lakshmana encounter the powerful demoness Tataka, who torments the sages and disrupts their spiritual practices. Rama, utilizing his exceptional archery skills, defeats Tataka and frees the sages from her terror. This act of bravery solidifies Rama's reputation as a skilled warrior.

Impressed by Rama's prowess, Vishwamitra decides to take Rama and Lakshmana to Mithila, where King Janaka is organizing a great ceremony called the Sita Swayamvar. The highlight of the ceremony is the challenge of lifting and stringing the formidable bow of Lord Shiva, known as the Shiva Dhanush. The feat is considered impossible for ordinary mortals.

Upon reaching Mithila, Rama is awestruck by the grandeur of the city and the magnificence of the Swayamvar. Princes and noble warriors from various kingdoms have gathered to win the hand of Sita, King Janaka's daughter. The atmosphere is charged with anticipation and excitement.

Rama, with humility and grace, approaches the sacred bow and effortlessly lifts it, causing a collective gasp from the assembled guests. As he prepares to string the bow, it suddenly snaps into two with a resounding sound, shattering the hopes of the other contenders. The breaking of Shiva's bow signifies Rama's unmatched strength and divine intervention.

The breaking of Shiva's bow not only confirms Rama's eligibility as a suitor but also solidifies his divine nature and purpose. It is a symbol of his chosen path and the extraordinary destiny that lies ahead of him. The incident also showcases the power of Lord Shiva, as the breaking of the bow signifies his approval of Rama as a suitable match for Sita.

King Janaka, recognizing the divine significance of this event, offers his daughter Sita's hand in marriage to Rama. The announcement is met with joy and celebration among the guests and the citizens of Mithila. Rama's marriage to Sita marks the union of two souls destined to embark on a monumental journey that will shape the course of history.

The breaking of Shiva's bow and Lord Rama's marriage is not merely a story of love and matrimony but also a tale of divine intervention, destiny, and the triumph of righteousness. It symbolizes the union of two noble souls brought together by divine will. Rama's strength and skill, coupled with the breaking of the bow, signify his extraordinary qualities as a warrior and a leader.

Moreover, the breaking of Shiva's bow and Rama's marriage is a significant turning point in the Ramayana. It marks the beginning of Rama and Sita's shared destiny, their trials, and their ultimate victory over the forces of evil. Their union becomes the embodiment of love, devotion, and righteousness, inspiring generations to come.

In essence, the breaking of Shiva's bow and Lord Rama's marriage is a pivotal event in the Ramayana, symbolizing the divine intervention, valor, and destiny that shape the epic and set the stage for the extraordinary journey that unfolds. This event not only establishes Lord Rama as an exceptional warrior but also highlights his divine nature and purpose.

The breaking of Shiva's bow signifies Rama's unmatched strength and skill, as well as his eligibility as a suitor for Sita. It is a testament to his divine lineage and the favor bestowed upon him by the gods. The sound of the bow snapping reverberates through the air, shattering the hopes of the other contenders and leaving Rama as the undisputed victor.

Moreover, the breaking of Shiva's bow serves as a divine confirmation of Rama's chosen path and his ultimate destiny to defeat the forces of evil. It signifies the approval of Lord Shiva himself, highlighting Rama's divine purpose and the support he receives from the celestial realms.

The breaking of Shiva's bow also emphasizes the significance of the marriage between Rama and Sita. It is not just a union of two individuals but a union of souls destined to embark on a monumental journey. Rama's strength and valor, symbolized by the breaking of the bow, complement Sita's unwavering devotion and righteousness. Together, they form a formidable pair, ready to face the challenges that lie ahead.

Furthermore, the breaking of Shiva's bow and Rama's marriage hold deep cultural and symbolic meanings. It represents the triumph of good over evil, the victory of righteousness over injustice. It showcases the power of divine intervention and the importance of divine favor in the course of human lives. It teaches us that when we are aligned with our true purpose and guided by divine forces, we can overcome any obstacle and fulfill our destined roles.

The breaking of Shiva's bow and Lord Rama's marriage is a turning point in the Ramayana, propelling the narrative forward and setting the stage for the epic battles, trials, and triumphs that follow. It represents the beginning of Rama and Sita's shared journey, their unwavering commitment to righteousness, and their unbreakable bond of love and devotion.

As readers delve into the Ramayana, the breaking of Shiva's bow and Lord Rama's marriage serve as a reminder of the divine intervention and destiny that shape our lives. It encourages us to recognize the power within us, to embrace our divine purpose, and to face challenges with courage and determination.

In conclusion, the breaking of Shiva's bow and Lord Rama's marriage is a pivotal event in the Ramayana that symbolizes divine intervention, valor, and destiny. It sets the stage for the epic tale that unfolds, showcasing the remarkable qualities of Lord Rama and establishing the foundation for his heroic journey. This event captures the essence of the Ramayana, reminding us of the timeless wisdom and profound teachings embedded within this ancient epic.

CHAPTER THREE

Exile in the Forest

LORD RAMA'S EXILE AND HIS JOURNEY TO THE FOREST

Lord Rama's exile and his journey to the forest is a significant and transformative phase in the epic Ramayana. It is a period of profound challenges, self-discovery, and spiritual growth that shapes Lord Rama's character and reveals the depth of his devotion, resilience, and righteousness.

The exile of Lord Rama begins with the unfortunate turn of events when Kaikeyi, one of King Dasharatha's wives, demands that Rama be sent into exile for fourteen years and that her own son Bharata be crowned as the king of Ayodhya. Bound by his sense of duty and honor, Rama willingly accepts his father's decree and prepares himself for the journey ahead.

With his devoted wife Sita and his loyal brother Lakshmana by his side, Lord Rama embarks on a profound journey into the forest. The forest becomes the backdrop for their trials and tribulations, offering both physical and spiritual challenges that test their character and fortitude.

During their exile, Lord Rama encounters various sages, mystics, and celestial beings who impart invaluable wisdom and guidance. They provide him with spiritual teachings, guidance on dharma (righteousness), and insights into the true nature of existence. Lord Rama embraces these teachings with humility and gratitude, deepening his understanding of his divine purpose and strengthening his resolve to fulfill his duties as a warrior, prince, and devotee.

The forest also serves as a crucible for Lord Rama's character development. It is here that he confronts his inner demons, battles with temptation, and demonstrates unwavering devotion to his principles. He faces formidable adversaries, such as the demon king Ravana's allies, who test his physical prowess and mental strength. Through these encounters, Lord Rama exhibits extraordinary bravery, strategic thinking, and righteous action, establishing himself as an embodiment of virtue and dharma.

The journey through the forest is not just a physical one but also a spiritual pilgrimage. Lord Rama's exile becomes an opportunity for self-reflection and introspection, allowing him to deepen his connection with the divine and strengthen his spiritual resolve. He seeks solace in meditation, engages in devotional practices, and fosters a profound relationship with nature. The forest becomes a sacred space where he encounters the mystical and divine, further fueling his spiritual growth and awakening.

Lord Rama's exile is also a testament to his unwavering love and devotion to his wife Sita. Despite the challenges they face, including Sita's abduction by Ravana, Lord Rama remains steadfast in his commitment to rescuing her. His relentless pursuit and unwavering faith become a source of inspiration for generations to come, symbolizing the power of love and the triumph of good over evil.

Moreover, Lord Rama's journey through the forest teaches us valuable lessons about detachment, resilience, and surrender to the divine will. He embraces the transient nature of worldly attachments and focuses on his divine duty rather than personal desires. His journey serves as a reminder that true strength and fulfillment come from aligning oneself with a higher purpose and surrendering to the divine plan.

In conclusion, Lord Rama's exile and his journey through the forest in the Ramayana is a transformative phase filled with challenges, spiritual growth, and profound insights. It highlights Lord Rama's unwavering devotion, righteousness, and resilience in the face of adversity. His journey serves as a guiding light, inspiring us to embrace our own trials and tribulations with grace and unwavering faith, knowing that they are opportunities for personal and spiritual growth.

LIFE IN THE FOREST AND ENCOUNTER WITH VARIOUS DEMONS

Life in the forest and Lord Rama's encounters with various demons during his exile in the Ramayana are filled with suspense, action, and profound teachings. These episodes not only showcase Lord Rama's valor and strategic prowess but also impart valuable life lessons about facing challenges, overcoming inner demons, and staying true to one's purpose.

As Lord Rama, Sita, and Lakshmana navigate through the dense forests and sacred groves, they encounter a diverse array of beings, both human and non-human. Some of the most notable encounters include battles with demons such as Maricha, Subahu, Kabandha, and the formidable Surpanakha.

Maricha, a shape-shifting demon, attempts to disrupt Lord Rama's peaceful life in the forest by assuming the form of a golden deer, luring Sita away from their hermitage. Lord Rama recognizes the illusion and pursues the deer, eventually slaying Maricha with his arrow. This encounter teaches us about the importance of discernment and the need to resist temptations that distract us from our true path.

Another significant encounter is with the demoness Surpanakha, who is attracted to Lord Rama and attempts to seduce him. However, Lord Rama firmly rejects her advances, causing her to become enraged and attack Sita. In response, Lakshmana intervenes and cuts off Surpanakha's nose and ears. This incident serves as a powerful reminder of the importance of boundaries, respecting personal space, and standing up against harassment.

Lord Rama's encounter with Kabandha, a monstrous demon, is particularly intriguing. Kabandha reveals his true form and requests Lord Rama's help in attaining liberation from his cursed existence. Lord Rama agrees and fulfills Kabandha's wish by burning his body with a divine arrow, allowing him to ascend to the celestial realms. This episode highlights the transformative power of selfless acts and the potential for redemption even in the most unlikely beings.

Throughout their journey in the forest, Lord Rama, Sita, and Lakshmana also come across numerous sages and hermits who provide them with spiritual guidance and blessings. These encounters serve as reminders of the importance of seeking wisdom from enlightened beings and the transformative impact of their teachings on the path of self-realization.

Life in the forest not only tests Lord Rama's physical strength but also challenges him mentally and emotionally. The solitude and simplicity of the forest provide a fertile ground for introspection and self-reflection. Lord Rama embraces this opportunity by engaging in deep contemplation, meditation, and self-inquiry. His experiences in the forest deepen his connection with his inner self and strengthen his resolve to fulfill his divine purpose.

Moreover, the forest becomes a place of solace and sanctuary, offering Lord Rama and his companions moments of respite amidst their arduous journey. The beauty of nature, the melodious songs of birds, and the whispering of trees provide a sense of tranquility and remind them of the divine presence that permeates all of creation.

The encounters with various demons also serve as allegories for the inner battles and challenges that individuals face in their own lives. Each demon embodies a specific negative trait or tendency that humans must overcome. Lord Rama's victories over these demons signify the triumph of virtue, righteousness, and self-mastery over negative influences and destructive tendencies.

These episodes in the forest not only add excitement and adventure to the narrative but also offer profound teachings about courage, determination, and the power of righteousness. Lord Rama's encounters with demons teach us the importance of self-discipline, emotional control, and inner strength when facing the trials and tribulations of life.

Ramayana are an integral part of the epic's narrative, offering valuable insights and teachings that resonate with readers across generations. These episodes not only showcase Lord Rama's bravery and heroism but also delve deeper into the human experience, highlighting the inner battles we all face and the transformative power of righteousness.

The forest becomes a backdrop for Lord Rama's personal growth and spiritual journey. It serves as a testing ground where he must confront and overcome his own limitations, fears, and desires. The encounters with demons symbolize the challenges and temptations that arise in our own lives, urging us to stay true to our values and dharma.

Through his encounters with demons such as Maricha, Surpanakha, and Kabandha, Lord Rama exemplifies virtues such as discernment, self-control, and compassion. His unwavering commitment to righteousness and duty guides him in making the right choices and facing adversity with grace and strength.

Each encounter in the forest holds a profound lesson. Maricha's deceitful guise as the golden deer reminds us of the transient nature of material temptations and the importance of staying focused on our higher goals. Surpanakha's pursuit of Lord Rama serves as a cautionary tale about the destructive consequences of unchecked desires and the need to establish healthy boundaries.

Kabandha's liberation exemplifies the transformative power of selfless acts and the potential for redemption. Lord Rama's willingness to listen and assist him in attaining salvation reminds us of the importance of empathy, forgiveness, and the potential for growth and transformation, even in the most challenging circumstances.

These encounters also highlight the support and guidance Lord Rama receives from sages and hermits along his journey. Their wisdom and blessings serve as a reminder of the importance of seeking counsel from wise and enlightened individuals on our own paths of self-discovery.

The forest itself becomes a metaphor for the inner landscape of the human mind and soul. It represents a space of introspection, contemplation, and self-realization. Lord Rama's time in the forest allows him to delve into his own depths, to connect with his inner self, and to cultivate a deeper understanding of his purpose and divine nature.

Furthermore, the forest teaches us about the interconnectedness and interdependence of all beings. Lord Rama's interactions with animals, birds, and other forest dwellers emphasize the need for harmony and respect for all living creatures. It reminds us of the profound bond that exists between humans and nature and the responsibility we have to protect and preserve the natural world.

The episodes in the forest also demonstrate Lord Rama's unwavering commitment to dharma and righteousness. Despite the challenges and hardships he faces, he remains steadfast in his principles, acting as a role model for individuals seeking to lead a virtuous and meaningful life.

In essence, the episodes of Lord Rama's life in the forest and his encounters with various demons are rich with symbolism and teachings. They inspire us to reflect on our own inner struggles, to cultivate virtues such as courage, self-discipline, and compassion, and to stay aligned with our higher purpose even in the face of adversity.

The forest becomes a transformative space where Lord Rama undergoes profound growth and emerges as a true hero and exemplar of righteousness. His journey through the forest serves as a powerful reminder that our own struggles and challenges can be opportunities for self-discovery, personal growth, and the realization of our true potential.

The lessons learned from Lord Rama's experiences in the forest continue to resonate with readers, reminding us of the timeless wisdom and universal truths contained within the Ramayana. They invite us to reflect on our own lives, to navigate our own forests, and to strive for inner transformation and the fulfillment of our divine purpose.

CHAPTER FOUR

The Abduction of Sita

THE CUNNING PLAN OF RAVANA

The Ramayana is renowned for its portrayal of Ravana, the formidable antagonist and the king of Lanka. Ravana is a complex character who is known for his intelligence, power, and cunning nature. His role in the epic is crucial, as his actions set the stage for the ultimate conflict between good and evil.

Ravana, with his ten heads and unmatched strength, is driven by his desire for power and conquest. He is portrayed as a master strategist and a shrewd manipulator. The cunning plan of Ravana unfolds as he devises a scheme to abduct Sita, Lord Rama's beloved wife, in order to fulfill his own desires.

Ravana's plan begins with his sister, Surpanakha, who encounters Lord Rama and becomes enamored by his beauty. However, Lord Rama rejects her advances, which angers Surpanakha and triggers a chain of events. Seeking revenge, Surpanakha approaches Ravana and narrates the tale of Sita's unmatched beauty, igniting Ravana's desire to possess her.

Driven by his lust and ambition, Ravana formulates a meticulous plan to deceive and capture Sita. Disguised as a holy man, he approaches Sita in the absence of Lord Rama and his loyal brother, Lakshmana. Ravana uses his cunning words to deceive Sita, eventually revealing his true identity and forcefully abducting her.

The cunning plan of Ravana highlights his ability to manipulate and exploit situations to his advantage. He takes advantage of Sita's vulnerability and tests Lord Rama's devotion and determination. Ravana's actions not only disrupt the harmony and peace in Lord Rama's life but also set the stage for the epic battle that ensues.

However, it is important to note that while Ravana's plan is cunning and deceitful, it also serves a higher purpose in the grand narrative of the Ramayana. Ravana's actions act as a catalyst for the development of other characters, their strengths, and their unwavering commitment to righteousness. It allows Lord Rama to showcase his unwavering devotion to his wife and his determination to rescue her.

The cunning plan of Ravana also raises questions about the nature of good and evil. Ravana, despite being portrayed as the embodiment of evil, is a complex character with his own motivations and desires. His actions demonstrate the duality of human nature and the constant struggle between righteousness and temptation.

Ultimately, the cunning plan of Ravana serves as a turning point in the Ramayana. It propels the narrative forward and sets the stage for the epic battle between Lord Rama and Ravana. It tests the strength of character, faith, and love of the protagonists and underscores the triumph of righteousness over evil.

The cunning plan of Ravana serves as a reminder that intelligence and strategic thinking can be used for both noble and nefarious purposes. It emphasizes the importance of staying vigilant and steadfast in the face of deception and manipulation. The tale of Ravana's cunning plan is a timeless lesson that teaches us the consequences of succumbing to greed, lust, and the desire for power.

In conclusion, the cunning plan of Ravana is a pivotal element of the Ramayana that showcases his intelligence, manipulation, and thirst for power. It sets the stage for the ultimate clash between good and evil and tests the resolve and righteousness of the protagonists. The cunning plan of Ravana serves as a cautionary tale and a reminder of the eternal battle between darkness and light.

SITA'S ABDUCTION AND LORD RAMA'S SEARCH FOR HER

The abduction of Sita and Lord Rama's relentless search for her form a crucial and captivating narrative arc in the epic Ramayana. It is a tale of love, devotion, and unwavering determination that highlights the depths of Lord Rama's character and the strength of their bond.

The story begins with the cunning and deceitful Ravana, the king of Lanka, who becomes enamored by Sita's beauty and desires to possess her. Ravana formulates a plan and, disguised as a holy man, approaches Sita when she is alone in the forest.

Using his deceitful words, Ravana reveals his true identity and forcefully abducts Sita, taking her to his kingdom in Lanka.

Upon discovering Sita's abduction, Lord Rama, accompanied by his loyal brother Lakshmana, embarks on a relentless search to find his beloved wife. Their journey takes them through forests, mountains, and across vast expanses of land, as they encounter various sages, mystical beings, and creatures along the way.

Lord Rama's search for Sita is marked by unwavering determination, strength, and devotion. He faces numerous challenges and obstacles, but his love for Sita fuels his resolve to find her and bring her back. Lord Rama's journey becomes a symbol of the power of love and the lengths one is willing to go for their beloved.

During his search, Lord Rama receives guidance and assistance from various allies, including the wise and noble Hanuman, the monkey god. Hanuman's unwavering loyalty and his extraordinary abilities prove invaluable in Lord Rama's quest. Together, they gather an army of allies, including the Vanaras (monkey warriors) and other divine beings, to aid in their mission.

Lord Rama's search for Sita also becomes a test of his character and his commitment to righteousness. Along the way, he encounters ethical dilemmas, temptations, and challenges that put his integrity to the test. He stays true to his principles, upholding dharma (righteousness) even in the face of adversity.

The search for Sita takes Lord Rama and his allies to Lanka, the kingdom of Ravana. In a grand battle, they confront

Ravana and his army, engaging in fierce combat to rescue Sita. Lord Rama's unwavering determination, skill, and the support of his allies ultimately lead to the defeat of Ravana and the liberation of Sita.

The reunion of Lord Rama and Sita is a moment of immense joy and celebration. Their love and devotion to each other remain unwavering throughout the ordeal, demonstrating the power of their bond and the triumph of love over evil.

The tale of Sita's abduction and Lord Rama's search for her in the Ramayana holds several significant themes. It showcases the enduring power of love and the strength of character in the face of adversity. It also emphasizes the importance of dharma (righteousness), loyalty, and the unwavering pursuit of truth.

Moreover, the story of Sita's abduction and Lord Rama's search for her serves as a source of inspiration and reflection. It teaches valuable lessons about the consequences of actions, the importance of staying true to one's principles, and the indomitable power of love.

In conclusion, the abduction of Sita and Lord Rama's unwavering search for her form a central and captivating narrative in the Ramayana. It is a story of love, devotion, and the triumph of righteousness over evil. Lord Rama's relentless quest to find Sita serves as a timeless example of determination, courage, and the strength of their bond. The tale continues to resonate with readers, inspiring them to embrace love, uphold righteousness, and overcome challenges in their own lives.

CHAPTER FIVE

The Battle of Lanka

LORD RAMA'S ALLIANCE WITH HANUMAN AND THE VANARA ARMY

The alliance between Lord Rama and Hanuman, along with the mighty Vanara army, is a pivotal and awe-inspiring chapter in the epic Ramayana. It showcases the power of devotion, loyalty, and unity in the face of adversity, and highlights the extraordinary abilities and unwavering commitment of Hanuman and his fellow Vanaras.

Upon learning of Sita's abduction by the demon king Ravana, Lord Rama embarks on a quest to rescue her. During his journey, he encounters Hanuman, the loyal devotee of Lord Rama and the epitome of strength, wisdom, and devotion. Hanuman becomes an invaluable ally in Lord Rama's mission to reunite with Sita.

Hanuman's unwavering devotion and his extraordinary abilities make him an instrumental figure in the Ramayana. With his ability to fly, his immense strength, and his deep wisdom, Hanuman becomes an indispensable asset to Lord

Rama's cause. His dedication to serving Lord Rama and his unwavering loyalty make him a beloved character in Indian mythology.

Lord Rama and Hanuman form a deep bond of trust, respect, and friendship. Lord Rama recognizes Hanuman's unparalleled devotion and rewards him with his unwavering trust and love. Hanuman, in turn, pledges his life to Lord Rama's cause and becomes an embodiment of loyalty and selflessness.

As the quest to rescue Sita intensifies, Lord Rama and Hanuman embark on a series of extraordinary adventures together. Hanuman's devotion to Lord Rama and his unwavering determination to fulfill his mission make him a symbol of resilience and courage.

One of the most memorable episodes involving Lord Rama and Hanuman is the famous incident of Hanuman crossing the ocean in search of Sita. Lord Rama, unable to find a way to reach Lanka, seeks the help of Hanuman. In a remarkable display of his strength and devotion, Hanuman enlarges his form and leaps across the vast ocean, clearing every obstacle in his path. His dedication and determination inspire awe and admiration, as he demonstrates the lengths to which one can go in service of their beloved.

Upon reaching Lanka, Hanuman's encounter with Ravana showcases his extraordinary abilities and his unwavering commitment to Lord Rama. Hanuman's courage and wit enable him to outsmart and overpower Ravana's forces, creating chaos and confusion in Lanka.

The Vanara army, led by Hanuman, plays a crucial role in the battle against Ravana. The Vanaras, a race of powerful monkey warriors, possess incredible strength, agility, and strategic prowess. Their alliance with Lord Rama strengthens his cause and amplifies his chances of victory.

The Vanaras exhibit remarkable skills and demonstrate their loyalty to Lord Rama. With their ability to leap great distances, wield mighty weapons, and command the forces of nature, they prove to be invaluable allies in the quest to rescue Sita. Their fierce loyalty and unwavering commitment to Lord Rama serve as a testament to the power of unity and collective effort.

The alliance between Lord Rama, Hanuman, and the Vanara army represents the coming together of diverse beings for a common purpose. It exemplifies the strength that lies in unity, and the power that can be harnessed when individuals join forces to overcome challenges.

The camaraderie and unity within the alliance are evident throughout the epic. The mutual respect, trust, and support between Lord Rama, Hanuman, and the Vanaras foster a sense of brotherhood and create an unbreakable bond among them. Their shared goal of rescuing Sita drives them forward, and their combined efforts become a force to be reckoned with.

The alliance between Lord Rama, Hanuman, and the Vanara army culminates in the epic battle against Ravana and his forces. With Lord Rama's strategic guidance, Hanuman's unwavering devotion, and the Vanara army's formidable strength, they launch a full-scale assault on Lanka to rescue Sita and restore righteousness.

The battle is fierce and intense, with each side displaying their valor and prowess. Lord Rama, wielding his divine bow and arrows, showcases his exceptional combat skills and leadership. Hanuman, with his incredible strength and agility, becomes an unstoppable force on the battlefield, striking fear into the hearts of Ravana's warriors.

The Vanara army, united under the leadership of Hanuman, fights with unmatched ferocity and determination. Their ability to swiftly maneuver through the battlefield and their exceptional combat skills make them a formidable force. With their unwavering loyalty to Lord Rama and their deep sense of duty, they prove to be a crucial element in the final confrontation.

The battle reaches its climax as Lord Rama confronts Ravana in a one-on-one combat. With the blessings of the gods and the support of his allies, Lord Rama delivers a devastating blow to Ravana, ultimately slaying the demon king and liberating Sita from captivity.

The victory is not only a triumph over evil but also a testament to the power of righteousness, devotion, and unity. Lord Rama, Hanuman, and the Vanara army exemplify the qualities of true heroes who fight for justice and uphold the values of dharma.

The alliance between Lord Rama, Hanuman, and the Vanara army serves as a timeless example of the strength that can be derived from mutual trust, loyalty, and collaboration. It highlights the importance of standing united in the face of adversity and working together towards a common goal.

Beyond their military prowess, the alliance represents a deeper spiritual connection. Lord Rama, the embodiment of righteousness, represents the divine, while Hanuman symbolizes unwavering devotion and loyalty. Together, they inspire millions with their unwavering faith and determination.

The alliance's success in defeating Ravana and rescuing Sita not only restores harmony and justice but also serves as a beacon of hope for all who face challenges and adversity. It reminds us that with the right allies and a shared purpose, we can overcome any obstacle and achieve greatness.

The alliance between Lord Rama, Hanuman, and the Vanara army is celebrated and revered to this day. Their valor and heroism are commemorated in temples, scriptures, and cultural traditions, reminding people of the power of unity, courage, and faith.

The lessons learned from the alliance resonate beyond the pages of the Ramayana. They teach us the importance of forging strong alliances, cultivating unwavering devotion, and harnessing our collective strengths to overcome obstacles and achieve our goals.

As we reflect on the alliance between Lord Rama, Hanuman, and the Vanara army, let us draw inspiration from their remarkable journey. Let us remember that when we unite with others, remain steadfast in our convictions, and fight for what is right, we can overcome even the most formidable challenges and emerge victorious.

The alliance serves as a timeless reminder that when we come together, we become a force to be reckoned with. Just as Lord

Rama, Hanuman, and the Vanara army achieved greatness through their unity, so too can we accomplish remarkable feats when we stand together, united in purpose and bound by unwavering loyalty.

THE EPIC BATTLE WITH RAVANA AND THE VICTORY OF GOOD OVER EVIL

The epic battle with Ravana marks the climax of the Ramayana and is a powerful symbol of the victory of good over evil. It is a tale of bravery, determination, and divine intervention that captivates readers and teaches profound moral lessons.

The battle takes place in Lanka, the kingdom ruled by Ravana, a formidable demon king known for his immense power and cruelty. Lord Rama, accompanied by his loyal allies and the Vanara army, wages war against Ravana and his forces to rescue his beloved wife, Sita, who has been held captive by the demon king.

The stage is set for an epic confrontation between the forces of righteousness and the forces of evil. Lord Rama, the embodiment of virtue and righteousness, leads his army with unwavering resolve and divine guidance. His unwavering faith in dharma and his commitment to upholding truth and justice fuel his determination to defeat Ravana and restore peace and harmony.

Ravana, on the other hand, is a formidable adversary. He possesses immense physical strength and is supported by a vast army of demons. He is also protected by numerous divine boons and weapons. However, his arrogance and ego blind him to the righteousness of Lord Rama's cause and ultimately lead to his downfall.

The battle unfolds with both sides unleashing their most powerful weapons and strategies. Lord Rama's divine bow and arrows rain down upon Ravana's army, causing immense devastation. The Vanara army, led by the mighty Hanuman, showcases its extraordinary strength and agility, turning the tide of the battle in favor of righteousness.

The combat is fierce and relentless, with each side displaying their valor and skill. Heroes and demons clash, and the battlefield is filled with the clash of swords, the roar of mythical creatures, and the cries of victory and defeat. The fate of the world hangs in the balance as the forces of good and evil wage an epic struggle.

Throughout the battle, Lord Rama remains steadfast in his adherence to dharma. He never wavers in his commitment to righteousness, even in the face of seemingly insurmountable challenges. His unwavering faith in the divine and his unwavering love for Sita propel him forward, inspiring his allies and striking fear into the hearts of his enemies.

Divine interventions play a crucial role in the battle. Lord Rama receives guidance and blessings from various gods and goddesses, empowering him to overcome the obstacles before him. Hanuman, with his extraordinary powers, provides invaluable assistance, using his intellect and strength to turn the tide of the battle.

As the battle reaches its climax, Lord Rama and Ravana engage in a fierce one-on-one combat. Ravana, blinded by his own arrogance, underestimates Lord Rama's strength and determination. With a final arrow, Lord Rama pierces Ravana's heart, ending the reign of the demon king and liberating Sita from captivity.

The victory of Lord Rama over Ravana symbolizes the triumph of good over evil, righteousness over injustice, and light over darkness. It is a testament to the power of divine intervention and the unwavering resolve of those who fight for truth and justice. The battle serves as a moral lesson, reminding us of the importance of staying true to our principles and standing up against injustice.

Beyond its mythical and symbolic significance, the battle with Ravana teaches us valuable life lessons. It teaches us the importance of humility, as Ravana's downfall is ultimately caused by his arrogance and ego. It also emphasizes the power of unity and loyalty, as Lord Rama's allies and the Vanara army play vital roles in the victory.

The epic battle with Ravana is not only a thrilling tale of heroism and valor but also a profound allegory for the eternal struggle between good and evil in the world. It reflects the constant battle we all face within ourselves and in society, highlighting the choices we make and the consequences they bring.

Ravana, with his immense power and knowledge, represents the darker aspects of human nature such as ego, greed, and lust for power. His ten heads symbolize his multiple vices and the complexity of his evil character. On the other hand, Lord Rama embodies the qualities of righteousness, virtue, and selflessness.

His unwavering commitment to dharma and his adherence to moral principles make him a beacon of hope and inspiration.

The battle serves as a reminder that evil can never truly triumph over good, no matter how formidable it may seem. It illustrates that when individuals unite in the pursuit of justice and righteousness, they become a force to be reckoned with. Lord Rama's alliance with Hanuman and the Vanara army exemplifies the power of unity, cooperation, and collective effort in overcoming challenges.

Moreover, the battle with Ravana teaches us the importance of self-awareness and self-control. Ravana's downfall can be attributed to his inability to control his desires and his misguided sense of invincibility. In contrast, Lord Rama demonstrates the strength of character that comes from self-discipline, restraint, and moral clarity.

The epic battle also explores the themes of sacrifice and love. Lord Rama's unwavering devotion to Sita motivates him to confront Ravana and rescue her from captivity. His actions reflect the depth of his love and his willingness to go to great lengths to protect and reunite with his beloved. This highlights the power of love as a driving force for good and its ability to overcome even the most challenging obstacles.

Furthermore, the battle with Ravana showcases the importance of divine intervention and the role of faith in overcoming adversity. Lord Rama's unwavering faith in the divine and his belief that righteousness will prevail provide him with the strength and guidance needed to emerge victorious. The divine interventions throughout the battle serve as a reminder that there are greater forces at play and that we are not alone in our struggles.

The victory of Lord Rama over Ravana is not merely a triumph of one individual over another; it is a triumph of virtues over vices, of righteousness over wickedness. It instills in us the belief that, in the face of darkness, there is always a glimmer of hope. It encourages us to stand up against injustice, to fight for what is right, and to remain steadfast in our moral convictions.

The battle with Ravana serves as a timeless reminder that the fight between good and evil is not confined to mythological realms but is a constant battle within ourselves and in society. It inspires us to reflect on our own actions, values, and choices, urging us to choose the path of righteousness and virtue.

In conclusion, the epic battle with Ravana in the Ramayana is a captivating narrative that goes beyond its mythical and symbolic significance. It offers profound insights into the eternal struggle between good and evil, teaching us invaluable lessons about self-awareness, unity, sacrifice, love, and the power of faith. Through the inspiring journey of Lord Rama and the ultimate triumph of good over evil, we are reminded of the timeless values and principles that guide us in our own lives, encouraging us to strive for righteousness and contribute to a more just and harmonious world.

CHAPTER SIX

Return to Ayodhya

LORD RAMA'S RETURN TO AYODHYA WITH SITA

The return of Lord Rama to Ayodhya with Sita is a defining moment in the epic Ramayana, marking the culmination of a long and arduous journey filled with trials and tribulations. It is a joyous occasion that symbolizes the triumph of righteousness, the restoration of order, and the celebration of truth and justice.

After fourteen years of exile and the successful defeat of the demon king Ravana, Lord Rama prepares to return to his kingdom of Ayodhya. His victorious return is not just a personal triumph but also a significant event for the people of Ayodhya who eagerly await his arrival. The news of his homecoming spreads like wildfire, and the city is adorned with decorations and lit up with the glow of joy and anticipation.

As Lord Rama and Sita approach Ayodhya, the atmosphere is charged with excitement and reverence. The people of Ayodhya line the streets, eagerly waiting to catch a glimpse of their beloved prince and his virtuous consort. They shower flowers and offer prayers, expressing their gratitude for the safe return of their beloved prince and the restoration of righteousness in their kingdom.

The sight of Lord Rama and Sita on the chariot, adorned with divine garlands and surrounded by their loyal companions, evokes a sense of awe and reverence. The entire city is filled with the sounds of hymns, chants, and jubilant cries of "Jai Shri Ram" (Victory to Lord Rama), echoing the joy and relief that fills the hearts of the people.

The return of Lord Rama signifies not just the end of a period of exile but also the beginning of a new era of peace and prosperity. His leadership and commitment to justice inspire hope and confidence in the hearts of his subjects. Ayodhya, once again, becomes a haven of righteousness and harmony under the benevolent rule of Lord Rama.

The people of Ayodhya extend a warm welcome to Lord Rama and Sita, expressing their love, respect, and unwavering loyalty. They offer gifts, blessings, and heartfelt gratitude for the sacrifices made by the divine couple in upholding righteousness and protecting the values of dharma.

The return of Lord Rama is not just a personal triumph but also a moment of reconciliation and forgiveness. Lord Rama, ever the embodiment of compassion and righteousness, forgives those who had doubted him and embraced the path of darkness during his absence. He extends his hand of friendship and forgiveness, fostering unity and harmony among his subjects.

The streets of Ayodhya come alive with vibrant processions, music, and dance as the entire city celebrates the homecoming of their beloved prince. The atmosphere is filled with joy, love, and a sense of renewed hope for a brighter future under Lord Rama's righteous rule.

The return of Lord Rama and Sita also signifies the reunification of their divine love. Their separation during the exile was a test of their devotion and commitment to each other. Their reunion symbolizes the triumph of love over adversity and serves as an eternal example of devotion and fidelity.

The people of Ayodhya organize grand festivities and celebrations to honor the return of their beloved prince and his consort. Elaborate ceremonies, feasts, and cultural performances take place throughout the city, bringing together people from all walks of life to rejoice in the divine presence of Lord Rama and Sita.

The return of Lord Rama to Ayodhya with Sita is not just a historical event but a timeless lesson in righteousness, devotion, and the triumph of good over evil. It serves as a reminder of the importance of upholding moral values, standing up for justice, and leading a life guided by principles.

In conclusion, the return of Lord Rama to Ayodhya with Sita is a moment of immense joy, celebration, and spiritual significance in the epic Ramayana. It marks the culmination of a heroic journey filled with trials, tests, and triumphs, and represents the victory of righteousness and the restoration of order and harmony.

The return of Lord Rama and Sita to Ayodhya is not just a personal homecoming but a profound symbol of the triumph of good over evil. It signifies the fulfillment of their divine purpose and the ultimate realization of their destiny. Their return brings a sense of relief, joy, and renewed hope to the people of Ayodhya, who had eagerly awaited their beloved prince's return.

The people of Ayodhya express their love and devotion by decorating the city, lighting lamps, and offering prayers and gratitude for the safe return of their beloved prince and his virtuous consort. The streets are adorned with flowers, and the air is filled with chants, hymns, and the sounds of jubilant celebrations. The entire city comes alive with the spirit of unity, harmony, and reverence.

The return of Lord Rama and Sita is not just a reunion of a divine couple but a reaffirmation of their eternal love and unwavering commitment to each other. Their separation during the exile tested their devotion and strengthened their bond. Their reunion symbolizes the power of love, faith, and loyalty in overcoming all obstacles.

The return of Lord Rama also signifies the restoration of righteousness and the establishment of a just and righteous rule in Ayodhya. Lord Rama's exile and his subsequent return serve as a lesson in leadership, humility, and the pursuit of dharma. His reign brings prosperity, peace, and happiness to the people, as he governs with fairness, compassion, and wisdom.

The return of Lord Rama and Sita is not only a historical event but also holds profound spiritual significance. It reminds us of the eternal truth that righteousness will always prevail over evil, and that divine intervention is always at work, guiding and protecting those who walk the path of righteousness.

The return of Lord Rama and Sita is a celebration of the triumph of good, unity, and the victory of righteousness. It serves as a reminder that even in the face of adversity, one should remain steadfast in their principles and uphold the values of truth, justice, and compassion.

The Ramayana, through the narrative of Lord Rama's return, teaches us valuable lessons about love, devotion, righteousness, and the importance of staying true to one's values and purpose. It inspires us to persevere through challenges, to stand up for what is right, and to embrace the divine within ourselves.

In conclusion, the return of Lord Rama and Sita to Ayodhya is a moment of immense celebration and spiritual significance. It represents the triumph of good over evil, the restoration of righteousness, and the establishment of a just and harmonious rule. It reminds us of the eternal values of love, devotion, and righteousness, and inspires us to walk the path of dharma. The return of Lord Rama and Sita is a timeless story that continues to resonate with people, imparting valuable lessons and filling our hearts with joy, hope, and faith in the triumph of good.

CORONATION AND THE CELEBRATION OF VICTORY

The coronation and the celebration of victory in the Ramayana mark a significant milestone in the epic, representing the culmination of Lord Rama's heroic journey, the establishment of righteous rule, and the celebration of triumph over evil. It is a time of joy, festivity, and gratitude as Ayodhya rejoices in the return of their beloved prince and the dawn of a new era.

The coronation ceremony is a grand affair, filled with pomp and splendor. The city of Ayodhya is adorned with elaborate decorations, vibrant colors, and fragrant flowers. The streets are lined with enthusiastic onlookers, eagerly awaiting the sight of their revered prince being crowned as the rightful king. The air is filled with the sounds of music, chants, and the joyful voices of the people, expressing their love, admiration, and loyalty to Lord Rama.

As Lord Rama takes his rightful place on the throne, the atmosphere is charged with reverence and anticipation. The ceremony is conducted with great solemnity, invoking blessings from the divine and the ancestors. Priests perform sacred rituals, chanting hymns and mantras, symbolizing the divine sanction and the transfer of power. The crown is placed on Lord Rama's head, signifying his authority and responsibility as the ruler of Ayodhya.

The coronation is not merely a political event; it holds profound spiritual significance. Lord Rama's ascension to the throne represents the embodiment of righteous rule and the establishment of dharma. His reign signifies a just and compassionate governance, where the welfare of the people is prioritized, and the principles of truth, justice, and righteousness are upheld.

The celebration of victory is not limited to the coronation ceremony alone; it extends throughout the city and beyond. The entire kingdom comes alive with festivities, feasts, and cultural performances. People from all walks of life join in the celebrations, expressing their gratitude and joy for the restoration of peace, harmony, and righteousness.

The streets of Ayodhya are adorned with colorful processions, showcasing the rich cultural heritage of the kingdom. Musicians, dancers, and artists mesmerize the onlookers with their talent and skill, adding a sense of vibrancy and exuberance to the celebrations. The city resonates with the sounds of drums, cymbals, and joyful cheers, as the people come together to honor and celebrate their beloved prince and the victory of righteousness.

The celebration of victory is not limited to Ayodhya alone; it spreads across the entire realm. Messengers are sent to neighboring kingdoms, inviting them to join in the festivities and share in the joy of the triumph over evil. Kings, queens, and dignitaries from far and wide arrive in Ayodhya, bringing with them gifts, blessings, and good wishes for the newly crowned king.

The celebration also extends to the common people, who participate in various cultural and religious events organized throughout the kingdom. Temples are adorned with flowers and lights, and prayers are offered to the divine, expressing gratitude for the victory and seeking blessings for a prosperous and peaceful reign.

The celebration of victory is not just a momentary event; it signifies the beginning of a new chapter in Ayodhya's history. It heralds an era of prosperity, justice, and righteousness under the reign of Lord Rama. The people of Ayodhya look forward to a future filled with hope, where their beloved king will guide them on the path of righteousness and ensure their welfare and happiness.

In conclusion, the coronation and the celebration of victory in the Ramayana are significant events that mark the triumph of righteousness and the establishment of righteous rule. They are moments of immense joy, gratitude, and hope as Ayodhya rejoices in the return of their beloved prince and the dawn of a new era.

CHAPTER SEVEN

Lessons and Teachings from Ramayana

MORAL VALUES AND LIFE LESSONS FROM THE EPIC

The Ramayana, an ancient Indian epic, is not merely a story of heroism, adventure, and divine interventions; it is a treasure trove of moral values and life lessons that continue to resonate with readers across generations. Through the trials and tribulations faced by its characters, the Ramayana imparts profound wisdom and guidance on various aspects of life. Let us explore some of the moral values and life lessons that we can glean from this timeless epic.

UPHOLDING DHARMA

The Ramayana teaches us the importance of upholding dharma, or righteousness, in all our actions. Lord Rama, the epitome of righteousness, demonstrates unwavering commitment to his duties, even in the face of adversity. His actions remind us to prioritize moral and ethical values in our own lives.

LOYALTY AND DEVOTION

The loyalty and devotion displayed by characters like Hanuman and Sita highlight the virtues of unwavering commitment and selfless service. Hanuman's undying devotion to Lord Rama and Sita's unwavering loyalty to her husband serve as inspiring examples of true dedication and love.

RESPECT FOR PARENTS

Lord Rama's unwavering respect and obedience towards his parents, King Dasharatha and Queen Kaushalya, emphasize the importance of filial piety. The Ramayana reminds us of the sacred bond between parents and children and teaches us to honor and care for our parents.

SIBLING LOVE AND BONDING

The relationship between Lord Rama, Lakshmana, and Sita's brother, Bharata, showcases the importance of sibling love and loyalty. Despite the trials they face, their unwavering support and unconditional love for each other remain intact, highlighting the strength of familial bonds.

IMPORTANCE OF TRUTH AND HONESTY

The Ramayana emphasizes the significance of truth and honesty. Lord Rama's commitment to truth, even when it comes at a personal cost, serves as a powerful reminder of the importance of integrity in all aspects of life.

COURAGE AND BRAVERY

Characters like Lord Rama, Lakshmana, and Hanuman demonstrate extraordinary courage and bravery in the face of adversity. Their unwavering determination and fearlessness inspire us to overcome obstacles with courage and conviction.

FORGIVENESS AND COMPASSION

The Ramayana teaches us the power of forgiveness and compassion. Lord Rama's forgiveness towards his enemies, including Ravana, and his compassion towards those who seek his help exemplify the virtues of empathy and forgiveness.

IMPORTANCE OF SELF-CONTROL

The Ramayana highlights the significance of self-control and restraint. Lord Rama's ability to maintain his composure and make wise decisions, even in challenging circumstances, underscores the importance of self-discipline and self-mastery.

THE CONSEQUENCES OF PRIDE AND EGO

The characters of Ravana and Kaikeyi serve as cautionary examples of the destructive nature of pride and ego. Their actions and the consequences they face remind us of the need to keep our ego in check and avoid the pitfalls of arrogance.

THE POWER OF GOODNESS

The Ramayana portrays the triumph of good over evil. It instills in us the belief that goodness, righteousness, and virtue will ultimately prevail, even in the face of seemingly insurmountable challenges.

These moral values and life lessons from the Ramayana provide us with timeless wisdom and guidance. They serve as a compass, guiding us towards a righteous and meaningful life. As we immerse ourselves in the epic, we are reminded of the importance of upholding moral values, nurturing virtuous qualities, and striving for personal growth and spiritual evolution.

The Ramayana continues to be a source of inspiration and enlightenment, offering valuable insights into the complexities of human nature, the power of love, and the eternal struggle between good and evil. Its timeless teachings remind us of the importance of living a life of righteousness, compassion, and selflessness.

Through the trials and triumphs of its characters, the Ramayana teaches us that our actions have consequences and that our choices shape our destiny. It encourages us to be mindful of our thoughts, words, and deeds, as they have the power to impact not only our own lives but also the lives of those around us.

The epic also delves into the depths of human emotions and relationships, portraying the bonds of love, friendship, and loyalty. It teaches us the value of trust, communication, and understanding in nurturing and sustaining these relationships.

The Ramayana also imparts wisdom on the transient nature of material possessions and the importance of detachment. Lord Rama's renunciation of the royal comforts and his willingness to embrace a life of exile exemplify the notion that true fulfillment lies not in external circumstances but in the pursuit of inner virtues and spiritual growth.

Moreover, the Ramayana emphasizes the concept of divine intervention and the belief in a higher power. It highlights that even in the darkest of times, when all hope seems lost, faith and devotion can guide us towards light and salvation.

The epic's teachings extend beyond the realm of personal growth and encompass societal values as well. It emphasizes the need for a just and harmonious society where righteousness, justice, and compassion prevail. It underscores the responsibility of leaders to govern with integrity and serve the welfare of their subjects.

Furthermore, the Ramayana promotes the importance of environmental conservation and the harmonious coexistence of humans and nature. It showcases Lord Rama's reverence for all forms of life and his commitment to protecting the environment, serving as a reminder of our duty to be responsible custodians of the Earth.

In conclusion, the Ramayana continues to captivate hearts and minds with its profound moral values and life lessons. Its timeless teachings on righteousness, love, compassion, and the eternal struggle between good and evil hold relevance in today's world. By delving into the depths of human nature and relationships, it guides us towards leading a virtuous and purposeful life. As we embrace the wisdom of the Ramayana, we are inspired to navigate life's challenges with grace, uphold moral values, and strive for personal and spiritual growth.

RELEVANCE OF RAMAYANA IN MODERN TIMES

The Ramayana, an ancient epic, holds significant relevance in modern times. Despite being written thousands of years ago, its teachings, values, and themes continue to resonate with people across cultures and generations. Let us explore the relevance of the Ramayana in the context of contemporary society.

ETHICAL AND MORAL VALUES

The Ramayana embodies timeless ethical and moral values that are essential for personal and societal well-being. The virtues of truth, righteousness, loyalty, and integrity are emphasized throughout the epic. In today's world, where ethical dilemmas and moral challenges abound, the Ramayana serves as a guiding light, reminding individuals of the importance of living a life rooted in virtuous principles.

RELATIONSHIPS AND FAMILY DYNAMICS

The Ramayana explores various aspects of human relationships, including the bond between spouses, siblings, parents, and friends. It highlights the significance of trust, respect, and mutual support within these relationships. In an era marked by changing family structures and evolving social dynamics, the Ramayana offers insights into nurturing healthy and meaningful connections with loved ones.

LEADERSHIP AND GOVERNANCE

The Ramayana delves into the qualities of effective leadership and governance. Lord Rama, as an ideal king, embodies traits such as fairness, justice, compassion, and humility. The epic serves as a reminder to leaders in contemporary times to prioritize the welfare of their constituents, uphold moral values, and govern with integrity.

WOMEN EMPOWERMENT AND GENDER EQUALITY

The Ramayana features strong female characters like Sita, who exemplify resilience, courage, and wisdom. Despite the challenges they face, these women display remarkable strength and agency. The epic provides a platform to discuss women's empowerment and the importance of gender equality in modern society.

ENVIRONMENTAL STEWARDSHIP

The Ramayana showcases the deep reverence for nature and the environment. Lord Rama's connection with the natural world, as demonstrated during his time in the forest, highlights the need for ecological balance and sustainable practices. In an era of environmental degradation and climate change, the Ramayana's teachings on environmental stewardship are highly relevant.

INNER SELF AND SPIRITUALITY

The Ramayana delves into the realms of self-discovery, spirituality, and the quest for meaning in life. It explores the inner struggles and growth of characters, encouraging individuals to introspect, seek inner wisdom, and cultivate a deeper understanding of themselves. In today's fast-paced and materialistic world, the Ramayana offers a path towards self-realization and spiritual enlightenment.

UNITY AND DIVERSITY

The Ramayana celebrates the unity and diversity of India's cultural fabric. It brings together people from different regions, castes, and backgrounds, emphasizing the importance of harmony and inclusivity. In a globalized world marked by social and cultural divisions, the Ramayana serves as a reminder of the strength that lies in embracing diversity and fostering unity.

RESILIENCE AND PERSEVERANCE

The Ramayana portrays characters who face numerous challenges and adversities but emerge stronger through their resilience and perseverance. Their stories inspire individuals to overcome obstacles, face setbacks with determination, and find the inner strength to keep moving forward.

SOCIAL JUSTICE AND EQUALITY

The Ramayana raises important social justice issues, such as caste discrimination and the marginalization of certain groups. It highlights the need for a just society where every individual is treated with dignity and equality. In contemporary times, the Ramayana's messages on social justice remain pertinent, calling for the eradication of discrimination and the promotion of inclusivity.

Universal Themes of Love, Compassion, and Forgiveness: At its core, the Ramayana is a tale of love, compassion, and forgiveness. It portrays the triumph of love over hatred, the power of compassion to heal wounds, and the transformative nature of forgiveness. These universal themes resonate deeply with individuals across cultures and religions, reminding us of the importance of cultivating love, compassion, and forgiveness in our lives.

In modern times, where conflicts, animosity, and division prevail, the Ramayana's teachings on love, compassion, and forgiveness hold immense relevance. They encourage us to rise above our differences, embrace empathy, and foster a sense of unity and harmony.

Moreover, the Ramayana serves as a cultural and literary treasure that connects people to their heritage and roots. It provides a platform for intergenerational dialogue, allowing younger generations to learn about their cultural heritage and gain insights into the wisdom and values of their ancestors.

The Ramayana's relevance extends beyond its religious and cultural significance. Its timeless wisdom and profound insights into human nature make it a source of inspiration for individuals seeking guidance, solace, and meaning in their lives. It offers valuable lessons on personal growth, self-reflection, and the pursuit of righteousness.

Additionally, the Ramayana has influenced various art forms, literature, music, and performing arts, showcasing its enduring impact on the creative realm. Its characters, stories, and teachings continue to inspire artists and creators, fostering a rich artistic legacy.

In conclusion, the Ramayana's relevance in modern times cannot be overstated. Its teachings on ethical values, relationships, leadership, women empowerment, environmental stewardship, spirituality, and social justice offer valuable insights and guidance for navigating the complexities of contemporary life. It promotes unity, resilience, compassion, and the pursuit of higher ideals. As we delve into the epic, we discover a profound tapestry of human experiences and timeless wisdom that continues to illuminate our path and inspire us to lead meaningful and virtuous lives. The Ramayana stands as a testament to the enduring power of storytelling and the universality of its messages, serving as a guiding light for generations to come.

The Enduring Legacy of Ramayana

RAMAYANA AS A SOURCE OF INSPIRATION AND DEVOTION

The Ramayana, one of the most revered and beloved epics of Indian literature, holds a special place in the hearts of millions around the world. It is not just a story but a source of inspiration and devotion for countless individuals. The epic narrative of the Ramayana, attributed to the sage Valmiki, weaves together a tapestry of love, devotion, sacrifice, and divine intervention that continues to captivate and inspire people across generations.

At its core, the Ramayana is a story of the divine incarnation of Lord Vishnu in the form of Lord Rama, his journey through life, and the challenges he faces along the way. It portrays the ideals of righteousness, honor, and dharma, providing a moral compass for individuals seeking to lead a virtuous and purposeful life. The characters in the Ramayana, such as Lord

Rama, Sita, Hanuman, and Ravana, embody various virtues and vices, offering valuable lessons and insights into human nature and behavior.

For devotees of Lord Rama, the Ramayana holds deep religious and spiritual significance. It serves as a guide for leading a righteous life, cultivating devotion, and deepening one's connection with the divine. Through the stories and teachings in the Ramayana, devotees find solace, inspiration, and a pathway to spiritual growth.

The Ramayana is also celebrated through various forms of devotion and religious practices. Reciting the epic or listening to its verses, known as Ramayana path, is considered an act of devotion that brings blessings and divine grace. Devotees gather in temples, homes, and community spaces to chant, sing bhajans (devotional songs), and engage in kirtan (devotional music) dedicated to Lord Rama. These practices create an atmosphere of reverence and devotion, deepening the connection between the individual and the divine.

Furthermore, the Ramayana serves as a source of inspiration for individuals navigating the complexities of life. It offers valuable insights into relationships, ethics, leadership, and the pursuit of righteousness. The character of Lord Rama, known for his unwavering devotion to dharma and his adherence to principles, serves as a role model for individuals seeking guidance in their personal and professional lives. His love and devotion for Sita, his unwavering loyalty to his friends and allies, and his resilience in the face of adversity inspire individuals to embody similar qualities in their own lives.

The Ramayana also teaches the importance of selflessness and sacrifice. Lord Rama's selfless actions, such as his decision to exile himself from his kingdom to honor his father's word and his relentless pursuit to rescue Sita from captivity, exemplify the virtues of sacrifice and devotion. These qualities inspire individuals to prioritize the well-being of others and to act selflessly for the greater good.

In addition to its religious and moral significance, the Ramayana is a treasure trove of literary and artistic excellence. It has inspired countless adaptations, retellings, and interpretations in various languages and art forms. It has influenced literature, poetry, music, dance, theater, and visual arts across different cultures and regions. The characters, stories, and themes from the Ramayana continue to inspire artists, writers, and performers, fueling their creativity and contributing to the richness of human expression.

Devotees of the Ramayana often undertake pilgrimages to sacred sites associated with Lord Rama's life, such as Ayodhya, Chitrakoot, and Rameshwaram. These pilgrimages offer devotees an opportunity to immerse themselves in the divine energy and to deepen their devotion and connection with Lord Rama.

In conclusion, the Ramayana serves as a profound source of inspiration and devotion for millions of people worldwide. It offers guidance, solace, and a pathway to spiritual growth. The epic's teachings on righteousness, devotion, and the triumph of good over evil continue to resonate with individuals seeking meaning and purpose in their lives. Through the characters and their struggles, the Ramayana imparts valuable life lessons on virtues such as love, compassion, loyalty, and forgiveness. It teaches us the importance of upholding moral values and standing up against injustice.

Moreover, the Ramayana's relevance extends beyond religious and cultural boundaries. Its universal themes of love, family, honor, and the pursuit of truth have a timeless appeal that transcends time and place. The epic has been translated into numerous languages and has inspired adaptations and retellings in various forms of literature, art, and entertainment.

In today's fast-paced and often tumultuous world, the Ramayana serves as a guiding light, reminding us of the power of faith, devotion, and resilience. It encourages us to face life's challenges with courage and determination, just as Lord Rama did during his journey. The epic reminds us of the eternal struggle between good and evil and inspires us to choose the path of righteousness, even in the face of adversity.

Furthermore, the Ramayana offers valuable insights into the complexity of human relationships and the importance of maintaining harmony within families, friendships, and communities. The bond between Lord Rama and his loyal allies, such as Hanuman and Sugriva, exemplifies the strength and support that can be found in genuine connections. It teaches us the value of trust, loyalty, and teamwork in achieving our goals and overcoming obstacles.

The Ramayana also emphasizes the significance of self-discovery and self-realization. Lord Rama's journey to fulfill his dharma and attain spiritual enlightenment resonates with individuals seeking personal growth and fulfillment. It encourages introspection, self-reflection, and the quest for inner wisdom.

Moreover, the Ramayana serves as a reminder of the power of divine intervention and grace. It reinforces the belief that when we walk the path of righteousness, we are guided and protected by a higher force. This message of hope and divine assistance provides comfort and reassurance in times of difficulty and uncertainty.

In conclusion, the Ramayana continues to be a cherished and relevant epic that offers profound insights, moral guidance, and spiritual inspiration. Its teachings on righteousness, devotion, and the eternal struggle between good and evil remain pertinent in today's world. Whether as a religious scripture, a literary masterpiece, or a source of artistic expression, the Ramayana holds a special place in the hearts of individuals seeking wisdom, solace, and a deeper connection with the divine. It is a timeless source of inspiration that continues to guide and uplift those who embark on the journey of exploring its profound teachings and timeless wisdom.

THE CULTURAL IMPACT OF RAMAYANA IN INDIAN SOCIETY

The Ramayana holds a significant cultural impact in Indian society, shaping and influencing various aspects of art, literature, music, dance, theater, and religious practices. Its profound impact can be seen in the religious devotion, moral values, social norms, and artistic expressions of the Indian people.

One of the primary cultural impacts of the Ramayana is its role in shaping religious beliefs and practices. It is considered one of the two major ancient Hindu epics, alongside the Mahabharata. The epic's characters, stories, and teachings have become an integral part of Hindu mythology and religious rituals. Devotees recite hymns, chant mantras, and perform religious ceremonies based on the events and teachings of the Ramayana. The epic is also a source of inspiration for bhakti (devotional) traditions, where devotees express their love and devotion to Lord Rama through prayer, song, and storytelling.

The Ramayana's cultural impact extends beyond religious practices to influence literature and language. It has served as a rich source of inspiration for poets, scholars, and writers throughout history. Countless literary works have been based on the Ramayana, including retellings, adaptations, and interpretations in different regional languages of India. These literary works not only showcase the diversity and richness of Indian literature but also contribute to the preservation and promotion of the Ramayana's cultural significance.

Furthermore, the Ramayana has played a crucial role in shaping the moral fabric of Indian society. The epic's emphasis on virtues such as righteousness, loyalty, humility, and respect for elders has had a profound impact on the moral values upheld by generations of Indians. The characters of Lord Rama, Sita, Hanuman, and others serve as moral exemplars, inspiring individuals to emulate their noble qualities in their daily lives. The teachings of the Ramayana have influenced the social and ethical codes of conduct in Indian society, promoting harmony, justice, and compassion.

The impact of the Ramayana is also evident in various art forms. The epic has been a source of inspiration for Indian classical dance forms such as Bharatanatyam, Kathak, and Odissi. Dancers often portray episodes from the Ramayana through expressive movements and gestures, bringing the epic's stories to life on stage. Similarly, the Ramayana has influenced Indian classical music, with numerous compositions dedicated to its characters and events. The epic's melodies and verses have been incorporated into classical music performances, bhajans (devotional songs), and folk songs, creating a cultural resonance that connects people to their heritage.

The Ramayana has also had a significant impact on Indian theater and cinema. The epic has been adapted into plays, musicals, and street performances, captivating audiences with its timeless stories and moral messages. Countless films have been made based on the Ramayana, showcasing the epic's narratives and characters on the silver screen. These cinematic adaptations not only entertain but also contribute to the cultural identity and pride of Indian cinema.

In addition to its artistic impact, the Ramayana has influenced societal norms and values in Indian communities. The epic's teachings on family values, respect for elders, and the role of women have shaped the traditional Indian family structure and social dynamics. The character of Sita, with her loyalty, sacrifice, and strength, has become an idealized representation of Indian womanhood. The epic's portrayal of familial love and duty has influenced the concept of joint families and the intergenerational bonds prevalent in Indian society.

Moreover, the Ramayana has served as a unifying force, transcending regional, linguistic, and caste barriers in India. The epic's stories and characters are cherished and celebrated across different states and communities, fostering a sense of cultural unity and shared heritage.

GLOSSARY OF KEY TERMS

DEFINITIONS AND EXPLANATIONS OF IMPORTANT TERMS AND NAMES

In the epic Ramayana, there are several important terms and names that hold significant meanings and symbolize various aspects of the story and its characters. Understanding these terms and names is crucial for a deeper appreciation and comprehension of the epic's narrative and its underlying teachings. Let us explore some of these important terms and names and their explanations:

RAMAYANA

The term "Ramayana" itself refers to the epic poem that narrates the story of Lord Rama's life. It is derived from the names "Rama" and "ayana," meaning "journey" or "adventure." The Ramayana is attributed to the sage Valmiki and is considered one of the two major ancient Hindu epics.

RAMA

Lord Rama is the central protagonist of the Ramayana. He is the seventh avatar of Lord Vishnu, revered as the ideal king, husband, and human being. Rama represents righteousness, virtue, and the embodiment of dharma (righteousness). His character embodies noble qualities such as courage, compassion, and unwavering devotion to duty.

SITA

Sita is the wife of Lord Rama and plays a pivotal role in the Ramayana. She is an epitome of purity, loyalty, and devotion. Sita symbolizes the ideal woman, exemplifying strength, resilience, and unwavering love for her husband. Her character also represents sacrifice and unwavering faith in the face of adversity.

HANUMAN

Hanuman is a prominent character in the Ramayana, known for his unwavering devotion to Lord Rama. He is a vanara (monkey) who possesses immense strength, intelligence, and agility. Hanuman is revered for his loyalty, humility, and service to Lord Rama. He symbolizes unwavering devotion, selflessness, and the power of faith.

RAVANA

Ravana is the primary antagonist in the Ramayana, a powerful demon king with ten heads. He is depicted as a symbol of arrogance, ego, and wickedness. Ravana abducts Sita and becomes the central obstacle in Lord Rama's quest to rescue her. His character represents the negative forces of greed, lust, and desire for power.

AYODHYA

Ayodhya is the capital city of the kingdom ruled by King Dasharatha, Lord Rama's father. It is a symbol of a prosperous and righteous kingdom. Ayodhya represents an ideal society based on principles of justice, harmony, and righteousness. Lord Rama's return to Ayodhya after his exile signifies the restoration of order and the triumph of good over evil.

LANKA

Lanka is the kingdom ruled by Ravana, located across the ocean from mainland India. It is portrayed as a city of opulence and grandeur. Lanka represents a realm of darkness, where evil and vice prevail. Lord Rama's journey to Lanka signifies the confrontation between good and evil, ultimately leading to the liberation of Sita and the defeat of Ravana.

VANARAS

The vanaras are a group of monkey-like beings who ally themselves with Lord Rama in his quest to rescue Sita. Led by Hanuman, they possess unique abilities and contribute their strengths to Lord Rama's cause. The vanaras symbolize loyalty, unity, and the power of collective effort.

DHARMA

Dharma is a fundamental concept in Hindu philosophy and plays a central role in the Ramayana. It refers to righteousness, moral duty, and ethical principles that govern one's thoughts, actions, and responsibilities. The Ramayana emphasizes the importance of upholding dharma in personal and societal life. Ashram

Ashram refers to a hermitage or a residence where spiritual seekers, sages, and ascetics live. In the context of the Ramayana, ashrams serve as secluded sanctuaries in forests or remote locations, where sages and hermits dedicate themselves to spiritual practices, meditation, and the pursuit of knowledge. Ashrams are often depicted as places of peace, tranquility, and wisdom, where individuals can seek guidance, enlightenment, and spiritual growth.

AYURVEDA

Ayurveda is an ancient Indian system of medicine that focuses on holistic healing and maintaining a balance between the body, mind, and spirit. In the Ramayana, references to Ayurveda can be found in the healing practices and herbal remedies used by characters such as the sage Vishwamitra and the vanara army. Ayurveda emphasizes the importance of natural remedies, diet, lifestyle, and maintaining harmony with nature for overall well-being.

JATAYU

Jatayu is a noble and courageous vulture who plays a significant role in the Ramayana. He encounters Ravana during Sita's abduction and valiantly fights to save her. Although he is ultimately defeated by Ravana, his sacrifice and loyalty to Lord Rama symbolize selflessness and devotion.

VIBHISHANA

Vibhishana is Ravana's younger brother who recognizes the righteousness of Lord Rama's cause and defects from Ravana's side to join Lord Rama's army. Vibhishana represents the power of conscience and the ability to make moral choices, even in challenging circumstances. His character signifies the importance of aligning oneself with truth and righteousness.

AGNI PARIKSHA

Agni Pariksha refers to the trial by fire that Sita undergoes to prove her purity and loyalty to Lord Rama after her rescue from Lanka. It is a significant episode in the Ramayana that tests Sita's character and devotion. The Agni Pariksha highlights the ideals of purity, fidelity, and the expectation placed on women to prove their virtue in traditional societies.

VANAVASA

Vanavasa refers to the period of exile that Lord Rama, Sita, and Lakshmana spend in the forest. It represents a phase of detachment from worldly comforts and a journey of self-discovery and spiritual growth. Vanavasa teaches the characters the values of simplicity, resilience, and the ability to overcome hardships.

YAGNA

Yagna refers to a sacred ritualistic offering performed to invoke divine blessings and express gratitude to deities. In the Ramayana, yagnas are conducted by sages, kings, and divine beings as acts of worship and devotion. They symbolize the importance of gratitude, surrender, and the establishment of divine connections.

Understanding these terms and names enhances our comprehension of the Ramayana's teachings, symbolism, and cultural significance. The epic's rich tapestry of characters, events, and concepts continues to inspire and resonate with people across generations, serving as a timeless source of wisdom, morality, and spiritual guidance.

RECOMMENDED FURTHER READING

ADDITIONAL BOOKS AND RESOURCES FOR DEEPER EXPLORATION OF RAMAYANA

The Ramayana is a vast and profound epic that has inspired countless retellings, interpretations, and scholarly works over the centuries. For those seeking to delve deeper into the world of Ramayana, there are numerous books and resources available that offer insightful perspectives, detailed analyses, and engaging retellings of the epic. Here are some notable recommendations:

"RAMAYANA" BY VALMIKI

The original text by Sage Valmiki is a must-read for anyone interested in the Ramayana. It provides the foundational story and serves as the basis for all subsequent retellings and adaptations.

"THE RAMAYANA: A MODERN RETELLING OF THE GREAT INDIAN EPIC" BY RAMESH MENON

This modern retelling captures the essence of the Ramayana in a contemporary and accessible language. Menon's rendition retains the spirit and beauty of the original while making it more approachable for modern readers.

"RAMAYANA: DIVINE LOOPHOLE" BY SANJAY PATEL

This visually stunning book presents the Ramayana in a unique and captivating style. Patel's vibrant illustrations bring the characters and scenes to life, making it an engaging read for both children and adults.

"THE RAMAYANA: A SHORTENED MODERN PROSE VERSION OF THE INDIAN EPIC" BY R.K. NARAYAN

Renowned author R.K. Narayan offers a concise yet evocative retelling of the Ramayana, capturing the essence of the epic in a modern prose style. Narayan's storytelling prowess brings out the human drama and moral dilemmas of the characters.

"RAMAYANA: AN ILLUSTRATED RETELLING" BY ARSHIA SATTAR

This beautifully illustrated edition presents a concise retelling of the Ramayana accompanied by captivating artwork. Sattar's narrative skillfully distills the epic into its essential elements, making it an ideal choice for readers new to the Ramayana.

"RAMAYANA: DIVINE LOOPHOLE" BY KEVIN T. JOHN AND SANJAY PATEL

This graphic novel adaptation combines Kevin T. John's lyrical storytelling with Sanjay Patel's mesmerizing artwork. It offers a visually stunning and immersive experience, making the Ramayana accessible to readers of all ages.

"THE RAMAYANA: A MODERN ADAPTATION" BY LINDA EGENES AND KUMUDA REDDY

This contemporary adaptation of the Ramayana explores the universal themes of love, duty, and sacrifice. The authors infuse the story with modern sensibilities while staying true to the core teachings and values of the epic.

"THE VALMIKI RAMAYANA: CRITICAL ESSAYS" EDITED BY A. SHARMA

This collection of critical essays delves into various aspects of the Ramayana, including its literary, philosophical, and cultural significance. It offers scholarly insights and interpretations that deepen our understanding of the epic.

"RAMAYANA STORIES IN MODERN SOUTH INDIA: AN ANTHOLOGY" EDITED BY PAULA RICHMAN

This anthology brings together a collection of diverse and contemporary retellings of the Ramayana from different regions of South India. It highlights the regional variations and cultural nuances in the retelling of the epic.

"THE RAMAYANA: A NEW RETELLING OF VALMIKI'S ANCIENT EPIC" BY LINDA EGENES

In this retelling, Linda Egenes provides a fresh perspective on the Ramayana, drawing inspiration from various versions and interpretations. Her narrative style and insights offer a unique exploration of the epic.

These books offer a range of perspectives, styles, and interpretations of the Ramayana, allowing readers to explore different facets of the epic and delve deeper into its timeless wisdom. Whether you are a first-time reader or a seasoned enthusiast, these resources provide valuable insights and engaging narratives that will enrich your understanding and appreciation of the Ramayana. They offer diverse perspectives, from traditional retellings to modern adaptations, and scholarly analyses to artistic interpretations. By exploring these books, you can delve deeper into the profound themes, complex characters, and moral teachings that make the Ramayana a timeless epic.

In addition to books, there are other resources that can enhance your exploration of the Ramayana:

- Online Courses: Many platforms offer online courses on the Ramayana, taught by experts in the field. These courses provide in-depth knowledge, historical context, and critical analysis of the epic.
- Academic Journals and Research Papers: Academic journals dedicated to Indian literature and mythology often publish research papers and articles on the Ramayana. These scholarly works offer in-depth analysis and insights into various aspects of the epic.
- Documentaries and Films: There are several documentaries and films that explore the Ramayana from different perspectives. They provide visual interpretations and cultural insights that deepen our understanding of the epic.

- Cultural Festivals and Performances: Ramayana-based performances, such as traditional plays, dance-dramas, and musicals, are held in many parts of India and around the world. Attending these events can immerse you in the cultural heritage and artistic expressions associated with the Ramayana.

- Online Forums and Discussion Groups: Engaging in online forums and discussion groups dedicated to the Ramayana allows you to connect with fellow enthusiasts, share insights, ask questions, and explore different interpretations of the epic.

Remember, the Ramayana is a rich and multifaceted epic that has captivated generations with its timeless wisdom and compelling narrative. Each resource mentioned here offers a unique perspective and adds depth to your understanding of this revered text. Whether you prefer scholarly analyses, modern retellings, or artistic interpretations, these resources will guide you on a fascinating journey through the world of the Ramayana, unraveling its profound teachings and captivating stories.

So, embark on this literary adventure, dive into the pages of these books, and explore the vast landscape of the Ramayana. Discover the eternal truths, moral values, and cultural significance that continue to resonate in our lives. May your journey through the Ramayana be enlightening, inspiring, and transformative, as you uncover the timeless wisdom and beauty of this cherished epic.

The Untold Tales of Ayodhya

In this bonus chapter of "Ramayana: A Brief Retold Version of True Indian Mythology," we delve deeper into the rich tapestry of Ayodhya, the grand city where the legendary saga of Rama unfolds. We uncover some untold tales and explore the vibrant characters that inhabit this ancient realm.

THE GLORY OF AYODHYA

Ayodhya, the capital city of Kosala, stood resplendent on the banks of the Sarayu River. Known for its opulence and grandeur, the city was a testament to the prosperous reign of King Dasharatha. Magnificent palaces, sprawling gardens, and bustling marketplaces adorned the landscape, painting a picture of a thriving civilization.

The citizens of Ayodhya reveled in the benevolent rule of their king. The streets were abuzz with activity as merchants traded their wares, artists showcased their talents, and scholars engaged in intellectual pursuits. Ayodhya flourished under the wise governance of Dasharatha, fostering an atmosphere of harmony and prosperity.

THE COUNCIL OF SAGES

Within the palace walls, Dasharatha sought counsel from a revered council of sages. These wise seers, well-versed in the scriptures and endowed with divine knowledge, guided the king in matters of governance, spirituality, and the welfare of the kingdom.

Sage Vasishta, the chief advisor to the king, possessed immense wisdom and unparalleled insight. His serene presence and enlightened guidance were instrumental in shaping Dasharatha's decisions. Alongside Vasishta, the council included eminent sages like Kashyapa, Atri, Gautama, and Bharadwaja, each contributing their unique perspectives to the affairs of the kingdom.

The council of sages served as a moral compass for Dasharatha, ensuring that justice and righteousness prevailed throughout Ayodhya. Their wisdom and virtuous counsel were instrumental in maintaining the city's harmony and upholding the principles of dharma.

THE KINGDOM'S FESTIVALS

Ayodhya was renowned for its vibrant festivals, where the city would come alive with color, music, and celebration. These occasions served as a unifying force, bringing together people from all walks of life to honor their traditions and express their collective joy.

One such festival was the grand Navaratri celebration, a nine-night extravaganza dedicated to the worship of the divine feminine energy. Elaborate processions, mesmerizing dance performances, and devotional rituals took place throughout Ayodhya, immersing the city in a spiritual aura.

Another cherished festival was the coronation ceremony of the crown prince. The entire kingdom would rejoice as the heir to the throne was anointed amidst great pomp and splendor. The air would resonate with the sound of jubilant chants, and the streets would be adorned with vibrant decorations, symbolizing the kingdom's hope and anticipation for a prosperous reign.

AYODHYA'S UNSUNG HEROES

Amidst the grand narrative of Rama's journey, there were unsung heroes who played crucial roles in Ayodhya's tapestry. From the loyal guards who protected the city's gates to the humble artisans who crafted intricate works of art, Ayodhya thrived on the contributions of its diverse inhabitants.

The bards and storytellers of Ayodhya preserved the kingdom's rich heritage through their verses and recitations. Their mesmerizing performances transported the audience to distant realms, evoking emotions and fostering a sense of unity among the people.

The artisans of Ayodhya were masters of their crafts, weaving fabrics, sculpting statues, and creating intricate jewelry that adorned the city's nobility. Their artistry and dedication added beauty and elegance to Ayodhya's tapestry, showcasing the kingdom's rich cultural heritage.

AYODHYA'S LEGACY

As the epic tale of the Ramayana unfolds, it is essential to recognize the vibrant tapestry of Ayodhya. This bonus chapter sheds light on the city's grandeur, the wisdom of its sages, the vibrancy of its festivals, and the contributions of its unsung heroes. Ayodhya's legacy lives on, woven into the fabric of India's rich cultural heritage and serving as a reminder of the enduring values of righteousness, harmony, and devotion.

In Ayodhya, the soul of a great civilization thrived, creating a timeless saga that has inspired generations. Let us cherish and celebrate the magnificent city that set the stage for the extraordinary journey of Rama and continues to captivate hearts with its timeless charm.

OUR LATEST
RELEASED BOOKS

कहाँ पहुँचे आप?

जीवात्मा जगत और 7 चक्रों की यात्रा के रहस्य

राजीव सक्सेना

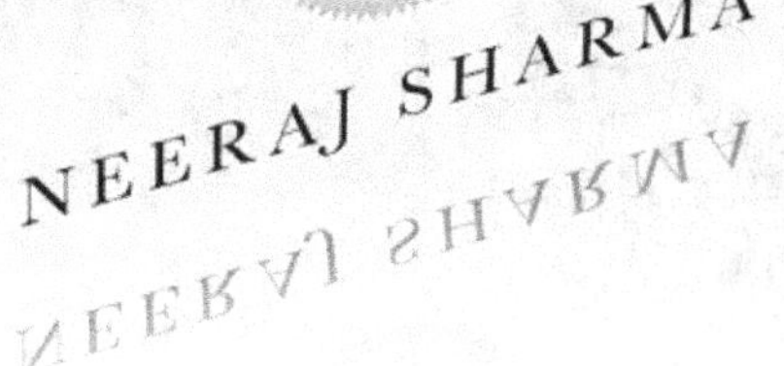

NEERAJ SHARMA

How to Write and Publish
YOUR OWN
BOOK
PRIYANKA "AABHAS"
YOUR OWN BOOK
PRIYANKA "AABHAS"

कैसे लिखें कैसे छापें
आपकी अपनी
किताब
प्रियंका "आभास"

UNLOCKING THE SECRETS TO AUTHORSHIP AND FINANCIAL SUCCESS

PUBLISH YOUR BOOK AND MAKE MONEY

A COMPLETE GUIDE FOR COACHES, TRAINERS, CONSULTANTS, SPEAKERS, ENTREPRENEURS, STUDENTS AND EVERYONE WHO WANTS TO SELF-PUBLISH A BOOK AND MARKET IT

YUKTI SHARMA

PUBLISH YOUR BOOK AND MAKE MONEY

YUKTI SHARMA

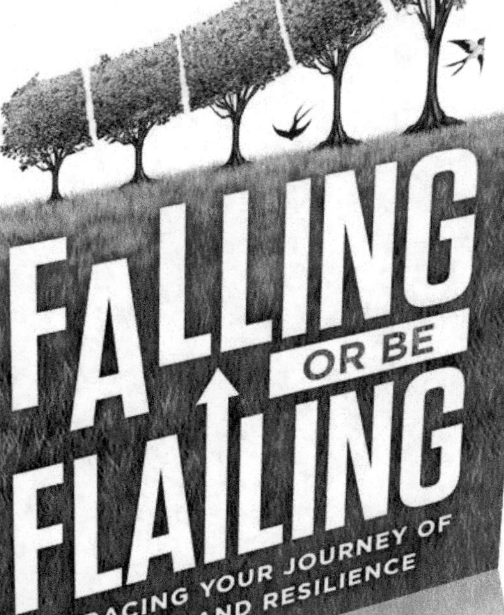

NEERAJ SHARMA
FALLING
OR BE
FLAILING
EMBRACING YOUR JOURNEY OF
GROWTH AND RESILIENCE
FALLING OR BE FLAILING
NEERAJ SHARMA

TOP SECRET ANCIENT
INDIAN SPIRITUAL KNOWLEDGE
UNLOCKING
The Secrets of
Breath
The Ultimate Life Changer
Embark on a Journey of
Self-Discovery Through Breath
RAJEEV SAXENA
UNLOCKING THE SECRETS OF BREATH
RAJEEV SAXENA

A GUIDE TO BECOMING AN
#1 NEW YORK TIMES BESTSELLER
THE ROAD TO
#1
Breaking #1 Bestseller Barriers
The Power of #1: Cracking the Code to Becoming a #1 Bestseller
DAKSH KAUSHIK
THE ROAD TO #1
DAKSH KAUSHIK

चक्रों को जाग्रत करने की संपूर्ण जानकारी और
साधना-विधियों की आसान गाइड

चक्र हीलिंग
चेंज योर लाइफ़
आपकी ऊर्जा शक्ति के 7 केंद्र

1 मूलाधार
2 स्वाधिष्ठान
3 मणिपूरक
4 अनाहत
5 विशुद्ध
6 आज्ञा
7 सहस्रार

बेस्टसेलर बुक्स
"सॉस के रहस्य"
के लेखक द्वारा

राजीव सक्सेना